OPPOSING
VIEWPOINTS®
SERIES

# Democracy

# Other Books of Related Interest:

## At Issue:

Does the World Hate the US?
Is Foreign Aid Necessary?
Weapons of War
What Is the Future of the US Economy?

## Current Controversies:

Developing Nations
Espionage and Intelligence
Patriotism
The Tea Party Movement

## Opposing Viewpoints:

America's Global Influence
Church and State
Dictatorships
The US Intelligence Community

# "Congress shall make no law ... abridging the freedom of speech, or of the press."

*First Amendment to the US Constitution*

The basic foundation of our democracy is the First Amendment guarantee of freedom of expression. The Opposing Viewpoints Series is dedicated to the concept of this basic freedom and the idea that it is more important to practice it than to enshrine it.

# Democracy

*David Haugen and Susan Musser, Book Editors*

**GREENHAVEN PRESS**
*A part of Gale, Cengage Learning*

Detroit • New York • San Francisco • New Haven, Conn • Waterville, Maine • London

GALE
CENGAGE Learning·

Elizabeth Des Chenes, *Managing Editor*

© 2012 Greenhaven Press, a part of Gale, Cengage Learning

Gale and Greenhaven Press are registered trademarks used herein under license.

For more information, contact:
Greenhaven Press
27500 Drake Rd.
Farmington Hills, MI 48331-3535
Or you can visit our Internet site at gale.cengage.com.

For product information and technology assistance, contact us at:

Gale Customer Support, 1-800-877-4253.
For permission to use material from this text or product, submit all requests online at www.cengage.com/permissions.

Further permissions questions can be emailed to permissionrequest@cengage.com.

Articles in Greenhaven Press anthologies are often edited for length to meet page requirements. In addition, original titles of these works are changed to clearly present the main thesis and to explicitly indicate the author's opinion. Every effort is made to ensure that Greenhaven Press accurately reflects the original intent of the authors. Every effort has been made to trace the owners of copyrighted material.

Cover Image © Lisa S./Shutterstock.com

**LIBRARY OF CONGRESS CATALOGING-IN-PUBLICATION DATA**

Democracy / David Haugen and Susan Musser, book editors
      p. cm. -- (Opposing viewpoints)
    Includes bibliographical references and index.
    ISBN 978-0-7377-5717-0 (hardback) -- ISBN 978-0-7377-5718-7 (paperback)
  1. Democracy--Juvenile literature. I. Haugen, David M., 1969- II. Musser, Susan.
    JC423.D381256 2012
    321.8--dc23

                                                                    2011047012

Printed in the United States of America
1 2 3 4 5 6 7 16 15 14 13 12

# Contents

## Chapter 3: What Should Be Done to Improve US Democracy?

## Chapter 4: Should the United States Foster Democracy Worldwide?

# Why Consider Opposing Viewpoints?

> "The only way in which a human being
> can make some approach to knowing
> the whole of a subject is by hearing
> what can be said about it by persons of
> every variety of opinion and studying
> all modes in which it can be looked at
> by every character of mind. No wise
> man ever acquired his wisdom in any
> mode but this."
>
> John Stuart Mill

In our media-intensive culture it is not difficult to find differing opinions. Thousands of newspapers and magazines and dozens of radio and television talk shows resound with differing points of view. The difficulty lies in deciding which opinion to agree with and which "experts" seem the most credible. The more inundated we become with differing opinions and claims, the more essential it is to hone critical reading and thinking skills to evaluate these ideas. Opposing Viewpoints books address this problem directly by presenting stimulating debates that can be used to enhance and teach these skills. The varied opinions contained in each book examine many different aspects of a single issue. While examining these conveniently edited opposing views, readers can develop critical thinking skills such as the ability to compare and contrast authors' credibility, facts, argumentation styles, use of persuasive techniques, and other stylistic tools. In short, the Opposing Viewpoints Series is an ideal way to attain the higher-level thinking and reading skills so essential in a culture of diverse and contradictory opinions.

In addition to providing a tool for critical thinking, Opposing Viewpoints books challenge readers to question their own strongly held opinions and assumptions. Most people form their opinions on the basis of upbringing, peer pressure, and personal, cultural, or professional bias. By reading carefully balanced opposing views, readers must directly confront new ideas as well as the opinions of those with whom they disagree. This is not to argue simplistically that everyone who reads opposing views will—or should—change his or her opinion. Instead, the series enhances readers' understanding of their own views by encouraging confrontation with opposing ideas. Careful examination of others' views can lead to the readers' understanding of the logical inconsistencies in their own opinions, perspective on why they hold an opinion, and the consideration of the possibility that their opinion requires further evaluation.

## Evaluating Other Opinions

To ensure that this type of examination occurs, Opposing Viewpoints books present all types of opinions. Prominent spokespeople on different sides of each issue as well as well-known professionals from many disciplines challenge the reader. An additional goal of the series is to provide a forum for other, less known, or even unpopular viewpoints. The opinion of an ordinary person who has had to make the decision to cut off life support from a terminally ill relative, for example, may be just as valuable and provide just as much insight as a medical ethicist's professional opinion. The editors have two additional purposes in including these less known views. One, the editors encourage readers to respect others' opinions—even when not enhanced by professional credibility. It is only by reading or listening to and objectively evaluating others' ideas that one can determine whether they are worthy of consideration. Two, the inclusion of such viewpoints encourages the important critical thinking skill of objectively evaluating an author's credentials and bias. This evaluation will illuminate an author's reasons for taking a particular stance on an issue and will aid in readers' evaluation of the author's ideas.

It is our hope that these books will give readers a deeper understanding of the issues debated and an appreciation of the complexity of even seemingly simple issues when good and honest people disagree. This awareness is particularly important in a democratic society such as ours in which people enter into public debate to determine the common good. Those with whom one disagrees should not be regarded as enemies but rather as people whose views deserve careful examination and may shed light on one's own.

Thomas Jefferson once said that "difference of opinion leads to inquiry, and inquiry to truth." Jefferson, a broadly educated man, argued that "if a nation expects to be ignorant and free . . . it expects what never was and never will be." As individuals and as a nation, it is imperative that we consider the opinions of others and examine them with skill and discernment. The Opposing Viewpoints Series is intended to help readers achieve this goal.

*David L. Bender and Bruno Leone,*
*Founders*

# Introduction

> *"No country can consider itself entirely*
> *democratic, even though there is*
> *no doubt about which countries are*
> *completely undemocratic. Democracy*
> *is an ideal model and our thinking*
> *should be organized around this central*
> *theme: how can we lower the barriers*
> *to democracy and strengthen the*
> *convictions without which democracy*
> *is no more than shadow theater?"*
>
> Alain Touraine, International
> Social Science Journal, *May 1991*

More than one global monitoring institution has noted that the number of democracies in the world has doubled since the end of the Cold War in the early 1990s. However, in the new millennium, a debate rages about whether those gains can be sustained and perpetuated or whether the tide of democratic change might be ebbing. To optimistic observers, the world appears on the cusp of new democratic growth given the 2010–2011 popular revolutions in the predominantly Arab lands of the Middle East and North Africa. Other analysts, though, believe the fervor surrounding the Arab uprisings masks the fact that several professed democracies in other parts of the world are suffering setbacks due to human rights abuses, subversions of the rule of law, and government curtailment of civil liberties. Thus, even after the fall of communism, the fate of liberal democracy seems uncertain in the twenty-first century.

In its annual survey titled "Freedom in the World," Freedom House, a pro-democracy monitoring and advocacy organization, claimed that twenty-five nations showed declines in democracy in 2010, a slightly rosier figure than the forty countries that displayed declines in 2009. Freedom House makes its assessments based on criteria that measure freedom of the press, free and fair electoral processes, judiciary authority and independence, the bargaining power of trade unions, and other such political and civic institutions inherent to functioning democracies. Using these measures, Freedom House noted declines primarily in sub-Saharan Africa, Asia, Latin America, and Eastern Europe. A few countries such as Djibouti and Ethiopia in Africa and the territory of Nagorno-Karabakh in Eurasia lost their "partly free" classification and fell to "not free" in 2010.

In a January 14, 2010, article, *The Economist* commented on the 2010 Freedom House report; the pessimistic tone could equally apply to the 2011 update. The magazine stated, "Taken as a whole, the findings suggest a huge turn for the worse since the bubbly mood of 20 years ago, when the collapse of Soviet communism, plus the fall of apartheid, convinced people that liberal democracy had prevailed for good." According to *The Economist*, the problem of democracy's decline is compounded by the arrogance of tyrants and the brazen repressive dictates of autocracies. "There is more evidence of authoritarians swapping tips," *The Economist* asserts, than there is of unfree or partly-free nations learning from Western liberal models. Most worrisome, the magazine attests, is that "semi-free countries, uncertain which direction to take, seem less convinced that the liberal path is the way of the future."

Larry Diamond, a professor of political science and sociology at Stanford as well as co-editor of *The Journal of Democracy*, made a similar assessment two years prior to *The Economist* piece. In a March 17, 2008, opinion column for the Real Clear Politics website, Diamond lamented the ebbing of the democratic tide that followed the collapse of the Soviet Union. "In a few short years," he averred, "the democratic wave has been slowed by a powerful authoritarian undertow, and the world has slipped into a democratic recession." Citing rigged elections, corruption, and strong-arming within countries claiming to be democracies, Diamond believes that, for many, liberal democracy has been a "superficial phenomenon, blighted by multiple forms of bad governance: abusive police and security forces, domineering local oligarchies, incompetent and indifferent state bureaucracies, corrupt and inaccessible judiciaries, and venal ruling elites who are contemptuous of the rule of law and accountable to no one but themselves." Some pundits question whether the United States may also be suffering from some of these symptoms. Another article from *The Economist*, this time from March 1, 2010, argues that, despite its reputation as a bastion of democracy, America is not receptive to new political parties, continually faces government corruption scandals, and has a justice system that appears weighted against racial minorities.

If democracy has experienced setbacks in recent years, not everyone agrees that it is in retreat. Writing in the Spring 2011 issue of the *Harvard International Review*, Monty G. Marshall, the founder of the Center for Systemic Peace and Societal-Systems Research Incorporated, points out that it was not until the 1990s that half the world's population inhabited free countries. Furthermore, Marshall reports that free countries control more than 90 percent of the global gross domestic product. "From a global perspective, then," he claims, "the end of the Cold War may be thought of as the beginning of a democratic transition, and the twenty-first century as the start of a New Democratic Order in world politics." The New Democratic Order Marshall envisions has nothing to do with Western nations foisting their ideals on their global neighbors and everything to do with pressure from within states to increase social integration and expand civic freedoms. "Democratization, then, is the process by which civil society asserts popular authority over the institutions of the state, and the consolidation of democracy is the process by which civil society learns to govern itself through the conflict management capacity of the state, without resort to force,"

Marshall argues. The state is an adaptive structure that gives way when citizens learn to cohere and communicate—through telecommunications or even free trade—to demand changes that, to Marshall, seem a natural part of a mutually beneficial, civil society. With several nations eschewing violence in favor of peaceful change (predicated on the notion that everyone has a stake in the benefits of democratic rule), the New Democratic Order may gain more adherents as countries realize the advantages of embracing popular sovereignty. Marshall is not blind to the fact that many nations undergo bloody revolutions to achieve regime change, but he claims violence usually does not lead to a more stable, representative form of government. Marshall simply acknowledges that—even if some backsliding occurs—more and more nations are opening themselves up to democratic reform.

In *Opposing Viewpoints: Democracy*, numerous analysts and commentators take up the debate surrounding the expansion or retrenchment of democracy in the twenty-first century. In the first chapter, What Is the State of Democracy Worldwide?, these experts contend with that notion directly. In the second chapter, Can There Be Democracy in the Middle East?, other voices debate the prospects of democratic change in the Arab world. The uprisings in Libya, Tunisia, and other Arab nations will test Marshall's theory that revolution does not necessarily bring freedom, but the United States and other Western powers are supporting regime changes in this region in the hope that democracy will take hold. The third and fourth chapters of this anthology examine the idealism of the United States and whether its supposed freedoms can or should be exported. The commentators in the third chapter, What Should Be Done to Improve US Democracy?, tackle potential abuses within and fixes to America's own brand of democracy. The fourth chapter, Should the United States Foster Democracy Worldwide?, brings together advocates and critics who debate the intentions of a government that, for example, is backing the overthrow of the autocracies mentioned in Chapter 2. Overall, *Opposing Viewpoints: Democracy* addresses the question of whether the new millennium will bear witness to a rise in global democracy, or whether that system—as it is practiced in the heart of the free world—is so flawed that it cannot permanently overturn autocratic governments or ensure such change will happen.

OPPOSING
VIEWPOINTS®
SERIES

# CHAPTER 1

# What Is the State of Democracy Worldwide?

# Chapter Preface

Since 1974, the world has lived through what Harvard political scientist Samuel P. Huntington terms the "third wave" of democracy. Beginning in countries like Spain, Portugal, Greece, and Brazil, the tide of democratic reform appeared strong in its initial stages. "During the following fifteen years," Huntington asserts, "this democratic wave became global in scope; about thirty countries shifted from authoritarianism to democracy, and at least a score of other countries were affected by the democratic wave." He claims that the relatively large number of countries in Latin America and Asia that embraced democratic government in the 1970s and 1980s constituted the bulk of the third wave, and this trend still seemed robust in 1991 when he published *The Third Wave: Democratization in the Late Twentieth Century*.

However Huntington acknowledges that the previous waves of democratization witnessed growth as well as setbacks. According to his theory, the first wave of democratization occurred in the mid-nineteenth century when America granted universal suffrage among white males, and the second wave followed the collapse of tyrannical regimes after World War II. Both periods experienced growth in the number of countries swearing allegiance to democratic principles inherent in popular, electoral government, but each period also tapered off and even underwent a reversal of fortune as supposed democracies were overthrown or turned despotic. Some observers believe the world is again suffering an ebb in democratization. Freedom House, a democracy advocacy group, reported early in 2011 that of 194 countries and fourteen territories monitored, only 115 professed electoral governments—a significant loss from 2005 when 123 countries defined themselves as democracies. In a January 13 press release, Freedom House added, "A total of 25 countries showed significant declines in 2010, more than double the 11 countries exhibiting noteworthy gains." Among the countries showing a decline were strife-ridden hot spots such as Iran and Afghanistan as well as less-obvious cases such as France and Mexico. Furthermore, the organization claimed that the Middle East and North Africa remain the regions exhibiting the least amount of democratic freedom.

These gloomy analyses, though, have not convinced everyone that democracy is in retreat. Since December 2010, several popular uprisings have rocked countries in the Arab world. From Tunisia and Egypt to Syria and Yemen, protests against oppressive governments have taken the form of strikes, street demonstrations, and social media campaigns. Libya embarked on a full-scale civil war in which a populace energized by a young, volunteer army sought—and achieved—the overthrow of longtime dictator Muammar Gadhafi. Writing in the February 18, 2011, edition of the *Chronicle of Higher Education*, history and political science teacher Richard Wolin remarked, "Never before have Arab citizens taken to the streets in such numbers, and with such persistence, to vent their displeasure with the political status quo." Building on Huntington's argument, Wolin questions whether the "Arab Spring" might be tantamount to a fourth wave of democracy—"a chain of loosely coordinated popular uprisings that, in years to come, will introduce the virtues of self-government to a region that, since decolonization, has known only the humiliations and indignities of authoritarian rule." With the successful ousting of Egyptian president Hosni Mubarak in February 2011 and the fight against Gadhafi before his assassination in October 2011, Wolin's assertion may not be unduly optimistic.

In the following chapter, several observers examine the state of democracy in the world in the first decade of the twenty-first century. Some believe the time and circumstances are favorable for an expansion of democratic ideals, while others maintain that serious impediments remain to real political change.

> "When the passion for freedom and democracy is ignited, neither the weight of . . . authoritarian rule nor the temptations of material wealth and economic progress can make them settle for anything less."

# Countries Around the World Are Striving to Establish Working Democracies

*Anwar Ibrahim*

*A former deputy prime minister of Malaysia, Anwar Ibrahim is currently a member of Malaysia's parliament and an outspoken advocate of free media and other democratic ideals in his country. The following viewpoint consists of Ibrahim's opening remarks at the 2010 Assembly of the World Movement for Democracy, an international collective of activists, educators, and policy makers that supports pro-democracy groups worldwide. In the viewpoint, Ibrahim utilizes the struggle toward more open democratic practices in Asia as an example of the momentum of pro-democracy trends in the late twentieth and early twenty-first centuries. According to Ibrahim, the taste of freedom has steeled the resolve of people in Indonesia and Kyrgyzstan, for instance, to accept nothing less than*

*democratic rule. He notes that the transition in these and other na-*
*tions embracing democracy will not be easy. Most of these diverse*
*lands have had to contend with religious and cultural clashes, but*
*Ibrahim believes that open democracy based on tolerance and plu-*
*rality can and must overcome these points of contention.*

As you read, consider the following questions:
1. According to Ibrahim, what argument do Asian autocrats most commonly make to suggest that their regimes
   are better suited than democracy to the interest of their
   countries?
2. How must democratic governments protect opposition
   parties to ensure democracy's participatory nature, in
   Ibrahim's opinion?
3. What role does Ibrahim attribute to the judiciary branch
   of government in the creation of a stable democracy?

On Tuesday [April 6, 2010], a people's revolt in Kyrgyzstan led by the opposition saw the government of President [Kurmanbek] Bakiyev crumble. The next day, about 3,000 people stormed the Parliament in Bangkok and occupied it for about two hours while thousands more occupied the capital's commercial district for a fifth day. This might or might not have led to a similar regime change but the imposition of martial law has put the matter at rest, at least for the moment. If we turn the clock back 60 years or so, we witness the Democrat Party winning an overwhelming victory in Turkey's first democratic election after decades of autocratic rule. This may be rather arbitrary but we could trace the seeds of this sea change to 1938, when the Turkish poet Nazim Hikmet was sentenced to twenty-eight years' jail after a sham trial held on a war ship. His poem, *The Epic of Sheik Bedreddin*, had fired an uprising in a classic case of solidarity across cultures, where Muslim, Christian, and Jewish Turks joined hands to fight oppression for the cause of freedom and democracy.

## Autocracy's Defiance

Nevertheless, there are still apologists, diehard skeptics and proponents of autocracy who say that democracy is not meant for all cultures because it is largely a Western construct and certainly not the only system for the rest of the world, let alone the best system. Asian values, for example, are said to be inherently incompatible with liberal democracy. The argument goes that the fundamental teachings of [the Chinese philosopher] Confucius place great importance on filial piety and submission to state authority. Democracy on the other hand goes the opposite direction by putting individual liberty ahead of the betterment of society.

The Asian values mantra of societal stability and paternalism were foisted on the people to drive home the message that authoritarian systems were better suited towards achieving certain economic objectives. Western notions of human rights and freedom were a stumbling block in the eradication of poverty and the path to modernization and global competitiveness. Indeed this ideology of a strong paternalistic government being the better alternative to liberal democracy appears to be gaining traction among certain leaders. Yes, we cannot deny that in the context of formulating a workable development model in Asia, authoritarian regimes appear to have chalked up some advances. The positive pointers are said to be in the areas of GDP [gross domestic product] growth, raising the standard of living and greater competitiveness in an increasingly globalized world, notwithstanding the challenges corruption, abject poverty seen in the gini coefficient data [a common measure of income inequality across nations] and marginalization of groups.

Thus, this begs the question: what price development?

We cannot deny too that in Asia, hardly three decades had passed before the euphoria of independence had been replaced with autocrats and dictators. As the concept of the rule of law was turned on its head, the guns of the law were turned on the

I was in Surabaya [Indonesia] in late January when I saw the news on television about the thousands of people protesting in the streets of Jakarta against President [Susilo Bambang] Yudhoyono. But he did not order troops to fire water cannons on the protesters or to use tear gas to break them up because in his words, "democracy means expressing opinions, thoughts, and criticism." And he advised the people to uphold the law and obey the Constitution.

So the Fourth Wave might well find its epicenter here in Indonesia. There is press freedom and elections are conducted freely and fairly. Significant changes are seen in areas of governance where the checks and balance are getting institutionalized. The judiciary may be mired in controversy but that is not borne by the complicity of the state. Rule of law generally prevails while institutions of power remain under the watchful eye of the anti-corruption agency. It is certainly no Utopia but as a nation emerging from three decades of dictatorship, I daresay that Indonesia is by far the most exemplary of nascent liberal democracies. And it is all the more remarkable considering that it is a predominantly Muslim nation in as much it completely demolishes the layers of prejudice built on the doctrine that Islam and democracy are diametrically opposed.

I would go further to say that the Indonesia phenomenon demonstrates that when the seeds of democracy are implanted in the hearts of the people, and when the passion for freedom and democracy is ignited, neither the weight of three decades of authoritarian rule nor the temptations of material wealth and economic progress can make them settle for anything less.

## The Requirements of a Functioning Democracy

There are still fundamental issues to be resolved because democracy may only serve as a façade for the aggrandizement of power and wealth through the back unless and until constitutional safeguards are put in place. And this must come hand in hand with good governance, transparency and accountability.

As opposed to sham democracies or autocracies in democratic skin, real democracies can only spring forth from elections that are free, fair and transparent. There must be a "level playing field". This means equal access to a free media, open debates and a conduct of elections that can stand up to scrutiny. Opposition parties and candidates must enjoy the freedom of speech, assembly, and movement necessary to voice their criticisms of the government openly and to bring alternative policies and candidates to the voters.

If democracy is participatory government in its fullest sense, then the existence of a vibrant opposition and civil society organizations is essential as the bulwark against the tyranny of absolute power, not be just merely tolerated but must be allowed to flourish as the people's conscience.

The rule of law and the protection of fundamental liberties are key features of a free and democratic society. To protect these basic rights, an independent judiciary is essential. Without one, there can be no effective check and balance against the powers of the executive and the legislative branches of government. If judges are to be independent of political authority, then their positions must be protected by the constitution. Appointments to high judicial office must also be transparent and done in the most scrupulous manner. Or what can we say about judicial impartiality when decisions in constitutional cases are as a matter of fact overturned by the appellate courts so as to favour the ruling political party? Under such circumstances, can we reasonably expect judges to protect citizens against governmental arbitrariness and political despotism?

It is therefore pertinent that we remind ourselves what this Fourth Wave of democratization must include for it to have any meaning. If we agree that a constitutional democracy must concern itself with the protection of minorities as well, government must ensure that their rights and liberties be not infringed even if it may entail the loss of popularity with the majority. Naturally this would entail making adjustments to overlapping claims to entitlement of rights or competing goals. Among the most significant of these competing claims is religion where history has shown that attempts by one community to impose its will on another will only lead to disharmony and eventual violence and bloodshed.

## Respecting Religion and Cultural Diversity

No doubt religious harmony can only be realized by making compromises from both sides. Leaders of democratic regimes must therefore not just attempt to play to the gallery or engage in grandstanding whenever the situation suits them. They must not blow hot and blow cold. They cannot on the one hand pride themselves as leading the way for cultural and ethnic harmony while on the other hand furtively stoke the fires of religious animosity through state-controlled media and other organs of propaganda.

At the heart of the matter, the balancing of minority interests with the majority requires ingenuous commitment from both sides as represented by their respective community leaders. Religious strife of whatever denomination or faith would seriously undermine the very foundation of constitutional democracy. There is therefore much sense in the saying that the empowerment of one cultural group at the expense of another in any society would only lead to a clash of interests. This clash if left unchecked would threaten the essential overlapping consensus, recognized as a central feature of the kind of democracy that we are talking about.

In the case of Asia, we can make her diversity in culture and religion a source of strength and richness, and the shared history of oppression and political enslavement, a further impetus to solidarity.

Yet there are still leaders who cling stubbornly to the belief that they need not heed the call for reform, freedom and democracy. There are still governments that are founded on the perpetuation of power not by free and fair elections but from arbitrary succession from the father to the son, or from one military clique to another, or even from one power elite to the next. And there are those who appear to have all the characteristics of a liberal democracy in so far as their domestic governance is concerned but they continue to violate human rights with impunity.

The rogue's gallery of such violators is staggering in sheer numbers. Indeed, to be truly meaningful, any talk of solidarity across cultures for the cause of freedom and democracy must take into account the serious human rights violations being perpetrated across the world. In this regard, where established multilateral institutions have failed in addressing these issues effectively, an alternative organization may be the answer. That would be one that is not beholden to any particular state, power or vested interest, and that is committed to take to task violators of human rights without fear or favour.

We can make diversity in culture and religion a source of strength and richness, and the shared history of oppression and political enslavement, a further impetus to solidarity. The flame that fires the passion for freedom and democracy must not be left to flicker, let alone die out. To keep it burning, we must remain resolute in our conviction to fight for freedom and democracy and defend it with courage, honour and dignity.

> "Semi-free countries, uncertain which direction to take, seem less convinced that the liberal path is the way of the future. And in the West, opinion-makers are quicker to acknowledge democracy's drawbacks."

# Countries Around the World Are Failing to Establish Working Democracies

## The Economist

The Economist *is a news journal published in the United Kingdom. The magazine refrains from giving author bylines, so the entire publication can speak with a unified voice. In the following viewpoint,* The Economist *claims that democracies tend to remain stable and weather economic and political misfortune better than their autocratic counterparts. However, the authors contend that tyrants still hold power in many nations, and in recent times, burgeoning democratic governments have fallen to repressive regimes. According to* The Economist, *one-party governments and despots of all kinds are arguing that democracy is not a road to prosperity and peace. Pointing to the military occupation of Iraq and Afghanistan as well as the economic dominance of China, various autocrats claim that democracy breeds discontent, division, and distraction. Although* The Economist *states that most people worldwide see the benefits of freedom offered by democracy, it also notes that some are afraid to give up the security they feel under regimented, repressive governments.*

As you read, consider the following questions:

1. According to the "Freedom in the World 2010" report, cited by the authors, how many countries experienced declines in liberty in 2009?
2. In *The Economist*'s view, how have the wars in Afghanistan and Iraq undermined democracy promotion worldwide?
3. As *The Economist* states, why does democracy generally fail to endure in non-market economies?

More than at any time since the Cold War, liberal democracy needs defending. That warning was issued recently by Arch Puddington, a veteran American campaigner for civil and political rights around the world.

This week [January 9–15, 2010] the reasons for his concern became clearer. Freedom House, a lobby group based in Washington, DC (where Mr. Puddington is research director), found in its latest annual assessment that liberty and human rights had retreated globally for the fourth consecutive year. It said this marked the longest period of decline in freedom since the organisation began its reports nearly 40 years ago.

Freedom House classifies countries as "free", "partly free" or "not free" by a range of indicators that reflect its belief that political liberty and human rights are interlinked. As well as the fairness of their electoral systems, countries are assessed for things like the integrity of judges and the independence of trade unions. Among the latest findings are that authoritarian regimes are not just more numerous; they are more confident and influential.

In its report entitled "Freedom in the World 2010: Global Erosion of Freedom", the American lobby group found that declines in liberty occurred last year in 40 countries (in Africa, Latin America, the Middle East and the ex-Soviet Union) while gains were recorded in 16. The number of electoral democracies went down by three, to 116, with Honduras, Madagascar, Mozambique and Niger dropping off the list while the Maldives were reinstated. This leaves the total at its lowest since 1995, although it is still comfortably above the 1990 figure of 69.

## The Trend Toward Democracy Twenty Years Ago

Taken as a whole, the findings suggest a huge turn for the worse since the bubbly mood of 20 years ago, when the collapse of Soviet communism, plus the fall of apartheid, convinced people that liberal democracy had prevailed for good. To thinkers like America's Francis Fukuyama, this was the time when it became evident that political freedom, underpinned by economic freedom, marked the ultimate stage in human society's development: the "end of history", at least in a moral sense.

In the very early days after the Soviet collapse, Russia and some of its neighbours swarmed with Western advisers, disseminating not only the basics of market economics but also the mechanics of multi-party democracy. And for a short time, these pundits found willing listeners.

Today, the idea that politicians in ex-communist countries would take humble lessons from Western counterparts seems laughable. There is more evidence of authoritarians swapping tips. In October, for example, the pro-Kremlin United Russia party held its latest closed-door meeting with the Chinese Communist party. Despite big contrasts between the two countries—not many people in Russia think there is a Chinese model they could easily apply—the Russians were interested by the Chinese "experience in building a political system dominated by one political party," according to one report of the meeting.

For freedom-watchers in the West, the worrying thing is that the cause of liberal democracy is not merely suffering political reverses, it is also in intellectual retreat. Semi-free countries, uncertain which direction to take, seem less convinced that the liberal path is the way of the future. And in the West, opinion-makers are quicker to acknowledge democracy's drawbacks—and the apparent fact that contested elections do more harm than good when other preconditions for a well-functioning system are absent. It is a sign of the times that a British reporter, Humphrey Hawksley, has written a book with the title: *Democracy Kills: What's So Good About the Vote?*

## Steering Clear of Western-Style Freedom

A more nuanced argument, against the promotion of electoral democracy at the expense of other goals, has been made by other observers. Paul Collier, an Oxford professor, has asserted that democracy in the absence of other desirables, like the rule of law, can hobble a country's progress. Mark Malloch-Brown, a former head of the UN Development Programme, is still a believer in democracy as a driver of economic advancement, but he thinks that in countries like Afghanistan, the West has focused too much on procedures—like multi-party elections—and is not open enough to the idea that other kinds of consensus might exist. At the University of California, Randall Peerenboom defends the "East Asian model", according to which economic development naturally precedes democracy.

Whatever the eggheads may be saying, there are some obvious reasons why Western governments' zeal to promote democracy, and the willingness of other countries to listen, have ebbed. In many quarters (including Western ones), the assault on Saddam Hussein's Iraq, and its bloody aftermath, seemed to confirm people's suspicion that promoting democracy as an American foreign-policy aim was ill-conceived or plain cynical.

In Afghanistan, the other country where an American-led coalition has been waging war in democracy's name, the corruption and deviousness of the local political elite, and the flaws of last year's election, have been an embarrassment. In the Middle East, America's enthusiasm for promoting democracy took a dip after the Palestinian elections of 2006, which brought Hamas to office. The European Union's "soft power" on its eastern rim has waned as enlargement fatigue has grown.

But perhaps the biggest reason why democracy's magnetic power has waned is the rise of China—and the belief of its would-be imitators that they too can create a dynamic economy without easing their grip on political power. In the political rhetoric of many authoritarian governments, fascination with copying China's trick can clearly be discerned.

For example, Syria's ruling Baath party talks of a "socialist market economy" that will fuel growth while keeping stability. Communist Vietnam has emulated China's economic reforms, but it was one of the states scolded by Freedom House this year for curbing liberty. Iran has called in Chinese legal experts and economists. There are limits to how much an Islamic republic and a communist state can have in common, but they seem to agree on what to avoid: Western-style freedom.

Even Cuba, while clinging to Marxist ideas, has shown an interest in China's economic reforms. And from the viewpoint of many poor countries, especially in Africa, co-operating with China—both economically and politically—has many advantages: not least the fact that China refrains from delivering lectures on political and human freedom. The global economic downturn—and China's ability to survive it—has clearly added to that country's appeal. The power of China (and a consequent lessening of official concern over human rights) is palpable in Central Asia. But as dissidents in the region note, it is not just Chinese influence that makes life hard for them; it is also the dithering of Western governments which often temper their moral concerns with commercial ones.

## Democracy's Best Arguments

Given that democracy is unlikely to advance, these days, through the military or economic preponderance of the West, its best hope lies in winning a genuinely open debate. In other words, wavering countries, and sceptical societies, must be convinced that political freedom works best.

So how does the case in defence of democracy stand up these days? As many a philosopher has noted, the strongest points to be made in favour of a free political contest are negative. Democracy may not yield perfect policies, but it ought to guard against all manner of ills, ranging from outright tyranny (towards which a "mild" authoritarian can always slide) to larceny at the public expense.

Transparency International, a corruption watchdog, says that all but two of the 30 least corrupt countries in the world are democracies (the exceptions are Singapore and Hong Kong, and they are considered semi-democratic). Autocracies tend to occupy much higher rankings on the corruption scale (China is somewhere in the middle) and it is easy to see why. Entrenched political elites, untroubled by free and fair elections, can get away more easily with stuffing their pockets. And strongmen often try to maintain their hold on power by relying on public funds to reward their supporters and to buy off their enemies, leading to a huge misallocation of resources.

Yet it is easy to find corrupt democracies—indeed, in a ramshackle place like Afghanistan elections sometimes seem to make things worse. Or take the biggest of the ex-Soviet republics. Russia is authoritarian and has a massive problem with corruption; Ukraine is more democratic—the forthcoming elections are a genuine contest for power, with uncertain results— but it too has quite a big corruption problem. Ukraine has no "Kremlin", wielding authority over all-comers, but that does not make it clean or well-governed.

What about the argument that economic development, at least in its early stages, is best pursued under a benign despot?

### The State of Democracy Worldwide

|  | No. of countries | % of countries | % of world population |
|---|---|---|---|
| Full democracies | 26 | 15.6 | 12.3 |
| Flawed democracies | 53 | 31.7 | 37.2 |
| Hybrid regimes | 33 | 19.8 | 14.0 |
| Authoritarian regimes | 55 | 32.9 | 36.5 |

Note. "World" population refers to the total population of the 167 countries covered by the index. Since this excludes only micro states, this is nearly equal to the entire actual estimated world population in 2010.

TAKEN FROM: Economist Intelligence Unit, *Democracy Index 2010: Democracy in Retreat*. New York: Economist Intelligence Unit, 2010.

Lee Kuan Yew, an ex-prime minister of Singapore, once asserted that democracy leads to "disorderly conduct", disrupting material progress. But there is no evidence that autocracies, on average, grow faster than democracies. For every economically successful East Asian (former) autocracy like Taiwan or South Korea, there is an Egypt or a Cameroon (or indeed a North Korea or a Myanmar) which is both harsh and sluggish.

The link between political systems and growth is hard to establish. Yet there is some evidence that, on average, democracies do better. A study by Morton Halperin, Joseph Siegle and Michael Weinstein for the Council of Foreign Relations (CFR), using World Bank data between 1960 and 2001, found that the average annual economic growth rate was 2.3% for democracies and 1.6% for autocracies. Other studies, though, are less clear.

Believers in democracy as an engine of progress often make the point that a climate of freedom is most needed in a knowledge-based economy, where independent thinking and innovation are vital. It is surely no accident that every economy in the top 25 of the Global Innovation Index is a democracy, except semi-democratic Singapore and Hong Kong.

China, which comes 27th in this table, is often cited as a vast exception to this rule. Chinese brainpower has made big strides in fields like computing, green technology and space flight. The determination of China's authorities to impose their own terms on the information revolution was highlighted this week when Google, the search engine, said it might pull out of China after a cyber-attack that targeted human-rights activists. Since entering the Chinese market in 2006, Google had agreed to the censorship of some search results, at the authorities' insistence.

Admirers of China's iron hand may conclude that it can manage well without the likes of Google, which was being trounced in the local market by Baidu, a Chinese rival. But in the medium term, the mentality that insists on hobbling search engines will surely act as a break on creative endeavour. And no country should imagine that by becoming as autocratic as China, it will automatically become as dynamic as China is.

## Democracy Breeds Stability

What about the argument that autocracy creates a modicum of stability without which growth is impossible? In fact, it is not evident that authoritarian countries are more stable than democracies. Quite the contrary. Although democratic politicians spend a lot of time vacillating, arguing and being loud and disagreeable, this can reinforce stability in the medium term; it allows the interests and viewpoints of more people to be heard before action is taken. On the State Fragility Index, which is produced annually by George Mason University and studies variables such as "political effectiveness" and security, democracies tend to do much better than autocracies. [Josip Broz] Tito's Yugoslavia [from 1953 to 1980] was stable, as was Saddam Hussein's Iraq—but once the straitjacket that held their systems together came off, the result was a release of pent-up pressure, and a golden opportunity for demagogues bent on mayhem.

At the very least, a culture of compromise—coupled with greater accountability and limits on state powers—means that democracies are better able to avoid catastrophic mistakes, or criminal cruelty. Bloody nightmares that cost tens of millions of lives, like China's Great Leap Forward or the Soviet Union's forced collectivisation programme, were made possible by the concentration of power in a small group of people who faced no restraint.

Liberal democratic governments can make all manner of blunders, but they are less likely to commit mass murder. Amartya Sen, a Nobel prize-winning economist, has famously argued that no country with a free press and fair elections has ever had a large famine. And research by those three CFR scholars found that poor autocracies were at least twice as likely as democracies to suffer an economic disaster (defined as a decline of 10% or more in GDP [gross domestic product] in a year). With no noisy legislatures or robust courts to hold things up, autocracies may be faster and bolder. They are also more accident-prone.

For all its frustrations, open and accountable government tends in the long run to produce better policies. This is because no group of mandarins, no matter how enlightened or well-meaning, can claim to be sure what is best for a complex society. Autocracies tend to be too heavy at the top: although decisions may be more easily taken, the ethos of autocracies—their secrecy and paranoia—makes it harder for alternative views to emerge. Above all, elections make the transfer of power legitimate and smooth. Tyrannies may look stable under one strongman; but they can slide into instability, even bloody chaos, if a transition goes awry. Free elections also mean that policy mistakes, even bad ones, are more quickly corrected. Fresh ideas can be brought in and politicians thrown out before they grow too arrogant.

## Political and Economic Tyranny Often Prevails

But if something has been learnt from the recent backlash against democratic enthusiasm, it is that ballot boxes alone are nothing like enough. Unless solid laws protect individual and minority rights, and government power is limited by clear checks, such as tough courts, an electoral contest can simply lead to a "tyranny of the majority", as Alexis de Tocqueville, a French philosopher, called it. That point has particular force in countries where some variety of political Islam seems likely to prevail in any open contest. In such places, minorities include dissident Muslims who often prefer to remain under the relative safety offered by a despot.

Another caveat is that democracy has never endured in countries with mainly non-market economies. The existence of an overweening state machine that meddles in everything can tempt leaders to use it against their political foes. Total control of the economy also sucks the air away from what Istvan Bibo, a Hungarian political thinker, called "the little circles of freedom"—the free associations and independent power centres that a free economy allows. Free-market economies help create a middle class that is less susceptible to state pressure and political patronage.

Perhaps most important, democracy needs leaders with an inclination and ability to compromise: what Walter Bagehot, a 19th-century editor of *The Economist*, called a "disposition rather to give up something than to take the uttermost farthing". Without a propensity for tolerating and managing differences, rival groups can easily reduce democracy to a ruthless struggle for power that ultimately wears down liberal institutions.

Democracy, this suggests, is more likely to succeed in countries with a shared feeling of belonging together, without strong cultural or ethnic fissures that can easily turn political conflict into the armed sort. Better positioned are "people so fundamentally at one that they can safely afford to bicker," as Lord Balfour, a 19th-century British politician, said. Such was not the case in Yugoslavia in the 1990s or in Lebanon in the 1970s.

Even where all the right conditions are in place, democracy will not prevail unless its proponents show success at governing. No constitution can, in itself, guarantee good governance. The success of any political system ultimately depends on whether it can provide basic things like security, wealth and justice. And in countries where experiments in democracy are in full swing, daily reality is more complex than either zealous democracy-promoters or authoritarian sceptics will allow.

In Kabul [Afghanistan] a 26-year-old handyman called Jamshed speaks for many compatriots when he lists the pros and cons of the new Western-imposed order. Compared with life under the Taliban, he appreciates the new "freedom to listen to music, to go out with your wife, to study or do whatever you want." But he cannot help remembering that "under the Taliban, you could leave your shop to pray and nobody would steal anything . . . now the government is corrupt, they take all your money."

Jamshed has never read [pro-democracy philosophers] John Stuart Mill or Ayn Rand. But whether he is ruled by theocrats or Western-backed election winners, he knows what he doesn't like.

*"The institutions, skills, and values needed to operate a free-market economy are those that, in the political sphere, constitute democracy."*

# Free Markets Foster Democracy

## Michael Mandelbaum

*In the following viewpoint, Michael Mandelbaum claims that free-market economies tend to embrace democracy more readily than closed, or government-run, economies. Mandelbaum states that this is because free markets protect private property, foster middle-class ideals, and create independent organizations such as trade unions that continue to promote and preserve the interests of individuals against government oppression. Although Mandelbaum asserts that free-market forces can influence governments to become more democratic, he warns that simply having a powerful economy is not a sign that a country will necessarily become a democracy. For this reason, Mandelbaum contends that the United States and other developed democracies must continue to promote freedom as well as market liberalism throughout the world. Michael Mandelbaum is a professor and the director of the American Foreign Policy program at The Johns Hopkins University.*

Michael Mandelbaum, "Democracy Without America: The Spontaneous Spread of Freedom," *Foreign Affairs*, vol. 86, no. 5, September/October, 2007, pp. 119–131. Reprinted by permission of FOREIGN AFFAIRS. Copyright 2007 by the Council on Foreign Relations, Inc. www.ForeignAffairs.com. All rights reserved. Reproduced by permission.

As you read, consider the following questions:

1. How does the creation of wealth implant democracy in free-market nations, according to Mandelbaum?
2. What two "habits" does Mandelbaum believe are both cultivated in free markets and central to democratic government?
3. As Mandelbaum asserts, why do Arab states that have economies based on oil revenues tend not to embrace democracy?

The administration of George W. Bush has made democracy promotion a central aim of U.S. foreign policy. The president devoted his second inaugural address to the subject, the 2006 National Security Strategy focused on spreading democracy abroad, and the White House has launched a series of initiatives designed to foster democracy across the globe, not least the military engagements in Afghanistan and Iraq. However, in Afghanistan, Iraq, and other parts of the Arab world where the prospects for democracy once seemed promising—Lebanon, the Palestinian territories, and Egypt—U.S. efforts have not succeeded. In none of these places, as the Bush administration enters its final 18 months in office, is democracy even close to being securely established. This is a familiar pattern. Virtually every president since the founding of the republic has embraced the idea of spreading the American form of government beyond the borders of the United States. The [Bill] Clinton administration conducted several military interventions with the stated aim of establishing democracy. Where it did so—in Somalia, Haiti, Bosnia, and Kosovo—democracy also failed to take root.

Yet the failure of Washington's democracy promotion has not meant the failure of democracy itself. To the contrary, in the last quarter of the twentieth century this form of government enjoyed a remarkable rise. Once confined to a handful of wealthy countries, it became, in a short period of time, the most popular political system in the world. In 1900, only ten countries were democracies; by midcentury, the number had increased to 30, and 25 years later the count remained the same. By 2005, fully 119 of the world's 190 countries had become democracies.

The seemingly paradoxical combination of the failure of U.S. democracy promotion and the successful expansion of democracy raises several questions: Why have the deliberate efforts of the world's most powerful country to export its form of government proved ineffective? Why and how has democracy enjoyed such extraordinary worldwide success despite the failure of these efforts? And what are the prospects for democracy in other key areas—the Arab countries, Russia, and China—where it is still not present? Answering these questions requires a proper understanding of the concept of democracy itself.

## Democratic Genealogy

What the world of the twenty-first century calls democracy is in fact the fusion of two distinct political traditions. One is liberty—that is, individual freedom. The other is popular sovereignty: rule by the people. Popular sovereignty made its debut on the world stage with the French Revolution, whose architects asserted that the right to govern belonged not to hereditary monarchs, who had ruled in most places at most times since the beginning of recorded history, but rather to the people they governed.

Liberty has a much longer pedigree, dating back to ancient Greece and Rome. It consists of a series of political zoning ordinances that fence off and thus protect sectors of social, political, and economic life from government interference. The oldest form of liberty is the inviolability of private property, which was part of the life of the Roman Republic. Religious liberty arose from the split in Christendom provoked by the Protestant Reformation of the sixteenth century. Political liberty emerged later than the other two forms but is the one to which twenty-first-century uses of the word "freedom" usually refer. It connotes the absence of government control of speech, assembly, and political participation.

Well into the nineteenth century, the term "democracy" commonly referred to popular sovereignty alone, and a regime based on popular sovereignty was considered certain to suppress liberty. The rule of the people, it was believed, would lead to corruption, disorder, mob violence, and ultimately tyranny. In particular, it was widely thought that those without property would, out of greed and envy, move to seize it from its owners if the public took control of the government.

At the end of the nineteenth century and the beginning of the twentieth, liberty and popular sovereignty were successfully merged in a few countries in western Europe and North America. This fusion succeeded in no small part due to the expansion of the welfare state in the wake of the Great Depression and World War II, which broadened the commitment to private property by giving everyone in society a form of it and prevented mass poverty by providing a minimum standard of living to all. Even then, however, the democratic form of government did not spread either far or wide.

Popular sovereignty, or at least a form of it, became all but universal by the second half of the twentieth century. The procedure for implementing this political principle—holding an election—was and remains easy. In the first three-quarters of the twentieth century, most countries did not choose their governments through free and fair elections. However, most governments could claim to be democratic at least in the sense that they differed from the traditional forms of governance—monarchy and empire. The leaders did not inherit their positions, and they came from the same national groups as the people they governed. These governments embodied popular sovereignty in that the people controlling them were neither hereditary monarchs nor foreigners.

If popular sovereignty is relatively easy to establish, the other component of democracy, liberty, is far more difficult to secure. This accounts for both the delay in democracy's spread around the world in the twentieth century and the continuing difficulties in establishing it in the twenty-first. Putting the principle of liberty into practice requires institutions: functioning legislatures, government bureaucracies, and full-fledged legal systems with police, lawyers, prosecutors, and impartial judges. Operating such institutions requires skills, some of them highly specialized. And the relevant institutions must be firmly anchored in values: people must believe in the importance of protecting these zones of social and civic life from state interference. . . .

## The Importance of a Free-Market Economy

The worldwide demand for democratic government in the modern era arose due to the success of the countries practicing it. The United Kingdom in the nineteenth century and the United States in the twentieth became militarily the most powerful and economically the most prosperous sovereign states. The two belonged to the winning coalition in each of the three global conflicts of the twentieth century: the two world wars and the Cold War. Their success made an impression on others. Countries, like individuals, learn from what they observe. For countries, as for individuals, success inspires imitation. The course of modern history made democracy seem well worth emulating.

The desire for a democratic political system does not by itself create the capacity for establishing one. The key to establishing a working democracy, and in particular the institutions of liberty, has been the free-market economy. The institutions, skills, and values needed to operate a free-market economy are those that, in the political sphere, constitute democracy. Democracy spreads through the workings of the market when people apply the habits and procedures they are already carrying out in one sector of social life (the economy) to another one (the political arena). The market is to democracy what a grain of sand is to an oyster's pearl: the core around which it forms.

The free market fosters democracy because private property, which is central to any market economy, is itself a form of liberty. Moreover, a successfully functioning market economy makes the citizens of the society in which it is established wealthier, and wealth implants democracy by, among other things, subsidizing the kind of political participation that genuine democracy requires. Many studies have found that the higher a country's per capita output, the more likely that country is to protect liberty and choose its government through free and fair elections.

Perhaps most important, the free market generates the organizations and groups independent of the government—businesses, trade unions, professional associations, clubs, and the like—that are known collectively as civil society, which is itself indispensable to a democratic political system. Private associations offer places of refuge from the state in which individuals can pursue their interests free of government control. Civil society also helps to preserve liberty by serving as a counterweight to the machinery of government. Popular sovereignty, the other half of modern democratic government, also depends on elements of civil society that the free market makes possible, notably political parties and interest groups.

Finally, the experience of participating in a free-market economy cultivates two habits that are central to democratic government: trust and compromise. For a government to operate peacefully, citizens must trust it not to act against their most important interests and, above all, to respect their political and economic rights. For governments to be chosen regularly in free elections, the losers must trust the winners not to abuse the power they have won. Likewise, trust is an essential element of markets that extend beyond direct local exchange. When a product is shipped over great distances and payment for it comes in installments that extend over time, buyers and sellers must trust in each other's good faith and reliability. To be sure, in a successfully functioning market economy, the government stands ready to enforce contracts that have been breached. But in such economies, so many transactions take place that the government can intervene in only a tiny fraction of them. Market activity depends far more on trust in others to fulfill their commitments than on reliance on the government to punish them if they fail to do so.

The other democratic habit that comes from participating in a market economy is compromise. Compromise inhibits violence that could threaten democracy. Different preferences concerning issues of public policy, often deeply felt, are inevitable in any political system. What distinguishes democracy from other forms of government is the peaceful resolution of the conflicts to which these differences give rise. Usually this occurs when each party gets some but not all of what it wants. Compromise is also essential to the operation of a market economy. In every transaction, after all, the buyer would like to pay less and the seller would like to receive more than the price on which they ultimately agree. They agree because the alternative to agreement is no transaction at all. Participants in a free market learn that the best can be the enemy of the good, and acting on that principle in the political arena is essential for democratic government.

## Promoting Free Markets Alone Is Not Enough

From this analysis it follows that the best way to foster democracy is to encourage the spread of free markets. Market promotion is, to be sure, an indirect method of democracy promotion and one that will not yield immediate results. Still, the rapid spread of democracy over the past three decades did exhibit a distinct association with free markets. Democracy came to the countries of southern Europe and Asia and to almost every country in Latin America after all of them had gained at least a generation's worth of experience, sometimes more, in operating market economies.

Viewed in this light, however, promoting democracy indirectly by encouraging the spread of free markets might seem unnecessary. Countries generally need no urging to recast their economies along free-market lines. Today, virtually all countries have done so, for the sake of their own economic growth. So important and so widespread had the goal of economic growth become in the second half of the twentieth century that the capacity to foster it had emerged as a key test of the political legitimacy of all governments. And the history of the twentieth century seemed to demonstrate conclusively that the market system of economic organization—and it alone—can deliver economic growth.

The free market, in this account, acts as a kind of Trojan horse. Dictatorships embrace it to enhance their own power and legitimacy, but its workings ultimately undermine their rule. Indeed, this line of analysis would seem to suggest not only that a foreign policy of deliberate market promotion is superfluous but that the ultimate triumph of democracy everywhere is assured through the universal voluntary adoption of free-market economic institutions and policies.

That, however, is not the case. The continued spread of democracy in the twenty-first century is no more inevitable than it is impossible, as is demonstrated by the decidedly varying prospects for this form of government in three important places where it does not exist: the Arab world, Russia, and China.

## Certain Strong Economies Can Resist Freedom

The prospects for democracy in the Arab countries are poor. A number of features of Arab society and political life work against it. None is exclusive to the Middle East, but nowhere else are all of them present in such strength. One of them is oil. The largest reserves of readily accessible oil on the planet are located in the region. Countries that become wealthy through the extraction and sale of oil, often called petro-states, rarely conform to the political standards of modern democracy. These countries do not need the social institutions and individual skills that, transferred to the realm of politics, promote democracy. All that is required for them to become rich is the extraction and sale of oil, and a small number of people can do this. They do not even have to be citizens of the country itself.

Furthermore, because the governments own the oil fields and collect all the petroleum export revenues, they tend to be large and powerful. In petro-states, the incentives for rulers to maintain control of the government are therefore unusually strong, as are the disincentives to relinquish power voluntarily. In these countries, the private economies, which elsewhere counterbalance state power, tend to be small and weak, and civil society is underdeveloped. Finally, the non-democratic governments of petro-states, particularly the monarchies of the Middle East, where oil is plentiful and populations are relatively small, use the wealth at their disposal to resist pressures for more democratic governance. In effect, they bribe the people they rule, persuading these citizens to forgo political liberty and the right to decide who governs them.

Arab countries are also unlikely candidates for democracy because their populations are often sharply divided along tribal, ethnic, or religious lines. Where more than one tribal, ethnic, or religious group inhabits a sovereign state in appreciable numbers, democracy has proved difficult to establish. In a stable democracy, people must be willing to be part of the minority. But people will accept minority status only if they feel confident that the majority will respect their liberty. In countries composed of several groups, such confidence is not always present, and there is little reason to believe it exists in Arab countries. The evidence of its absence in Iraq is all too clear.

For the purpose of developing democratic governments, Arab countries labor under yet another handicap. For much of their history, Arab Muslims saw themselves as engaged in an epic battle for global supremacy against the Christian West. The historical memory of that rivalry still resonates in the Arab Middle East today and fuels popular resentment of the West. This, in turn, casts a shadow over anything of Western origin, including the West's dominant form of government. For this reason, liberty and free elections have less favorable reputations in the Arab Middle East than elsewhere. In view of all these obstacles, whatever else may be said about the Bush administration, in aiming its democracy promotion efforts at the Arab world it cannot be accused of picking an easy target.

## Russia's Unstable Democratic Trend

The prospects for democracy in Russia over the next two to three decades are brighter. Russia today has a government that does not respect liberty and was not chosen through free and fair elections. The absence of democracy is due to the fact that seven decades of communist rule left the country without the social, political, and economic foundations on which democratic government rests. But Russia today does not confront the obstacles that barred its path to democracy in the past.

The communist political and economic systems have disappeared in Russia and will not be restored. Russia is also largely free of the historically powerful sense that the country had a cultural and political destiny different from those of other countries. Russia's population no longer consists, as it did until the industrialization and urbanization of the communist era, largely of illiterate peasants and landless agricultural workers. Today, the average Russian is literate, educated, and lives in a city—the kind of person who is eventually likely to find democracy appealing and dictatorship unacceptable. . . .

A countervailing force must be set against these harbingers of a more democratic future for Russia, however. The country's large reserves of energy resources threaten to tilt Russia in the direction of autocratic government. Post-Soviet Russia has the unhappy potential to become a petro-state. Russia's democratic prospects may therefore be said, with only modest exaggeration, to be inversely related to the price of oil.

## China's Powerful Ruling Party
## Resists Democracy

Of all the non-democratic countries in the world, the one where democracy's prospects matter most is China—the world's most populous country and one that is on course to have, at some point in the twenty-first century, the world's largest economy. The outlook for democracy in China is uncertain. Beginning in the last years of the 1970s, a series of reforms that brought many of the features of the free market to what had been a communist-style economy set in motion a remarkable quarter-century-long burst of double-digit annual economic growth. Although the core institution of a free-market economy, private property, has not been fully established in China, the galloping pace of economic growth has created a middle class. As a proportion of China's huge population it is small, but its numbers are increasing rapidly. More and more Chinese live in cities, are well educated, and earn a living in ways that provide them with both a degree of independence on the job and sufficient income and leisure time for pursuits away from work.

Along with the growth of the economy, the sorts of independent groups that make up civil society have proliferated in China. In 2005, 285,000 non-governmental groups were officially registered with the government—a tiny number for a country with a population of 1.3 billion—but estimates of the number of unofficial groups ran as high as eight million. Furthermore, twenty-first-century China emphatically fulfills one of the historical conditions for democracy: it is open to the world. Communist China's founding leader, Mao Zedong, sought to wall China off from other countries. His successors have opened the country's doors and welcomed what Mao tried to keep out.

The dizzying change that a quarter century of economic reform and its consequences have brought to China has therefore installed, in a relatively short period of time, many of the building blocks of political democracy. As Chinese economic growth proceeds, as the ranks of the country's middle class expand and civil society spreads, the pressure for democratic change is sure to increase. As it does, however, democracy advocates are just as certain to encounter formidable resistance from the ruling Chinese Communist Party (CCP).

Although it has abandoned the Maoist project of exerting control over every aspect of social and political life, the party remains determined to retain its monopoly on political power. It squelches any sign of organized political opposition to its rule and practices selective censorship. Explicit expressions of political dissent and any questioning of the role of the CCP are prohibited. Its efforts to retain power are not necessarily doomed to fail. The CCP has greater staying power than the ruling communist parties of Europe and the Soviet Union enjoyed before they were swept away in 1989 and 1991. Because it has presided over a far more successful economy than did its European and Soviet counterparts, the CCP can count on the tacit support of many Chinese who have no particular fondness for it and who do not necessarily believe it has the right to govern China in perpetuity without limits on its authority.

Popular indulgence of communist rule in China has another source: the fear of something worse. Recurrent periods of violence scar China's twentieth-century history. The Chinese people certainly wish to avoid further bouts of large-scale murder and destruction, and if the price of stability is the continuation of the dictatorial rule of the CCP, they may reckon that this is a price worth paying. The millions who have done particularly well in the quarter century of reform—many of them educated, cosmopolitan, and living in the cities of the country's coastal provinces—have reason to be wary of the resentment of the many more, mainly rural, residents of inland China whose well-being the economic boom has failed to enhance. The beneficiaries may calculate that CCP rule protects them and their gains. Finally, the regime can tap a widespread and potent popular sentiment to reinforce its position: nationalism. For example, it assiduously publicizes its claim to control Taiwan, a claim that seems to enjoy wide popularity on the mainland.

Whether, when, and how China will become a democracy are all questions to which only the history of the twenty-first century can supply the answers. Nonetheless, two predictions may be hazarded with some confidence. One is that if and when democracy does come to China—as well as to the Arab world and Russia—it will not be because of the deliberate and direct efforts at democracy promotion by the United States. The other is that pressure for democratic governance will grow in the twenty-first century whatever the United States does or does not do. It will grow wherever non-democratic governments adopt the free-market system of economic organization. Such regimes will adopt this system as part of their own efforts to promote economic growth, a goal that governments all over the world will be pursuing for as far into the future as the eye can see.

> *"Conventional wisdom holds that where either capitalism or democracy flourishes, the other must soon follow. Yet today, their fortunes are beginning to diverge."*

# Free Markets Threaten Democracy

### Robert B. Reich

*In the viewpoint that follows, Robert B. Reich claims that free markets are no guarantee of democratic government. Reich maintains that politicians and the public often put their faith in corporations to act in the interest of freedom and general welfare, but such trust has no foundation. He insists that corporations owe allegiance to investors and seek to maximize profits regardless of the social consequences. According to Reich, democratic principles should trump corporate interests, but he laments that even in free societies, the reverse is often the rule rather than the exception. Reich states that in order for the situation to change, the public must stop acting like investors with blind faith in free markets and recommit to the ideals and benefits of democracy over all. Robert B. Reich is a political economist who served as the secretary of labor under President Bill Clinton.*

As you read, consider the following questions:
1. As Reich states, what is capitalism's role in global society, and what is democracy's role?
2. Why does Reich believe most people are "of two minds" on the intersection of democracy and capitalism?
3. According to Reich, how do the Chinese elite secure their free-market gains in the absence of democracy?

It was supposed to be a match made in heaven. Capitalism and democracy, we've long been told, are the twin ideological pillars capable of bringing unprecedented prosperity and freedom to the world. In recent decades, the duo has shared a common ascent. By almost any measure, global capitalism is triumphant. Most nations around the world are today part of a single, integrated, and turbocharged global market. Democracy has enjoyed a similar renaissance. Three decades ago, a third of the world's nations held free elections; today, nearly two thirds do.

## Prosperous but Powerless Citizens

Conventional wisdom holds that where either capitalism or democracy flourishes, the other must soon follow. Yet today, their fortunes are beginning to diverge. Capitalism, long sold as the yin to democracy's yang, is thriving, while democracy is struggling to keep up. China, poised to become the world's third largest capitalist nation this year after the United States and Japan, has embraced market freedom, but not political freedom. Many economically successful nations—from Russia to Mexico—are democracies in name only. They are encumbered by the same problems that have hobbled American democracy in recent years, allowing corporations and elites buoyed by runaway economic success to undermine the government's capacity to respond to citizens' concerns.

Of course, democracy means much more than the process of free and fair elections. It is a system for accomplishing what can only be achieved by citizens joining together to further the common good. But though free markets have brought unprecedented prosperity to many, they have been accompanied by widening inequalities of income and wealth, heightened job insecurity, and environmental hazards such as global warming. Democracy is designed to allow citizens to address these very issues in constructive ways. And yet a sense of political powerlessness is on the rise among citizens in Europe, Japan, and the United States, even as consumers and investors feel more empowered. In short, no democratic nation is effectively coping with capitalism's negative side effects.

This fact is not, however, a failing of capitalism. As these two forces have spread around the world, we have blurred their responsibilities, to the detriment of our democratic duties. Capitalism's role is to increase the economic pie, nothing more. And while capitalism has become remarkably responsive to what people want as individual consumers, democracies have struggled to perform their own basic functions: to articulate and act upon the common good, and to help societies achieve both growth and equity. Democracy, at its best, enables citizens to debate collectively how the slices of the pie should be divided and to determine which rules apply to private goods and which to public goods. Today, those tasks are increasingly being left to the market. What is desperately needed is a clear delineation of the boundary between global capitalism and democracy—between the economic game, on the one hand, and how its rules are set, on the other. If the purpose of capitalism is to allow corporations to play the market as aggressively as possible, the challenge for citizens is to stop these economic entities from being the authors of the rules by which we live.

## The Cost of Doing Business

Most people are of two minds: As consumers and investors, we want the bargains and high returns that the global economy provides. As citizens, we don't like many of the social consequences that flow from these transactions. We like to blame corporations for the ills that follow, but in truth we've made this compact with ourselves. After all, we know the roots of the great economic deals we're getting. They come from workers forced to settle for lower wages and benefits. They come from companies that shed their loyalties to communities and morph into global supply chains. They come from CEOs who take home exorbitant paychecks. And they come from industries that often wreak havoc on the environment.

Unfortunately, in the United States, the debate about economic change tends to occur between two extremist camps: those who want the market to rule unimpeded, and those who want to protect jobs and preserve communities as they are. Instead of finding ways to soften the blows of globalization, compensate the losers, or slow the pace of change, we go to battle. Consumers and investors nearly always win the day, but citizens lash out occasionally in symbolic fashion, by attempting to block a new trade agreement or protesting the sale of U.S. companies to foreign firms. It is a sign of the inner conflict Americans feel—between the consumer in us and the citizen in us—that the reactions are often so schizophrenic.

Such conflicting sentiments are hardly limited to the United States. The recent wave of corporate restructurings in Europe has shaken the continent's typical commitment to job security and social welfare. It's leaving Europeans at odds as to whether they prefer the private benefits of global capitalism in the face of increasing social costs at home and abroad. Take, for instance, the auto industry. In 2001, DaimlerChrysler faced mounting financial losses as European car buyers abandoned the company in favor of cheaper competitors. So, CEO Dieter Zetsche cut 26,000 jobs from his global workforce and closed six factories. Even profitable companies are feeling the pressure to become ever more efficient. In 2005, Deutsche Bank simultaneously announced an 87 percent increase in net profits and a plan to cut 6,400 jobs, nearly half of them in Germany and

Britain. Twelve-hundred of the jobs were then moved to low-wage nations. Today, European consumers and investors are doing better than ever, but job insecurity and inequality are rising, even in social democracies that were established to counter the injustices of the market. In the face of such change, Europe's democracies have shown themselves to be so paralyzed that the only way citizens routinely express opposition is through massive boycotts and strikes.

## Left Behind by Economic Progress

In Japan, many companies have abandoned lifetime employment, cut workforces, and closed down unprofitable lines. Just months after Howard Stringer was named Sony's first non-Japanese CEO, he announced the company would trim 10,000 employees, about 7 percent of its workforce. Surely some Japanese consumers and investors benefit from such corporate downsizing: By 2006, the Japanese stock market had reached a 14-year high. But many Japanese workers have been left behind. A nation that once prided itself on being an "all middle-class society" is beginning to show sharp disparities in income and wealth. Between 1999 and 2005, the share of Japanese households without savings doubled, from 12 percent to 24 percent. And citizens there routinely express a sense of powerlessness. Like many free countries around the world, Japan is embracing global capitalism with a democracy too enfeebled to face the free market's many social penalties.

On the other end of the political spectrum sits China, which is surging toward capitalism without democracy at all. That's good news for people who invest in China, but the social consequences for the country's citizens are mounting. Income inequality has widened enormously. China's new business elites live in McMansions inside gated suburban communities and send their children to study overseas. At the same time, China's cities are bursting with peasants from the countryside who have sunk into urban poverty and unemployment. And those who are affected most have little political recourse to change the situation, beyond riots that are routinely put down by force.

But citizens living in democratic nations aren't similarly constrained. They have the ability to alter the rules of the game so that the cost to society need not be so great. And yet, we've increasingly left those responsibilities to the private sector—to the companies themselves and their squadrons of lobbyists and public-relations experts—pretending as if some inherent morality or corporate good citizenship will compel them to look out for the greater good. But they have no responsibility to address inequality or protect the environment on their own. We forget that they are simply duty bound to protect the bottom line.

## Entrusting Companies with Preserving the Public Good

Why has capitalism succeeded while democracy has steadily weakened? Democracy has become enfeebled largely because companies, in intensifying competition for global consumers and investors, have invested ever greater sums in lobbying, public relations, and even bribes and kickbacks, seeking laws that give them a competitive advantage over their rivals. The result is an arms race for political influence that is drowning out the voices of average citizens. In the United States, for example, the fights that preoccupy Congress, those that consume weeks or months of congressional staff time, are typically contests between competing companies or industries.

While corporations are increasingly writing their own rules, they are also being entrusted with a kind of social responsibility or morality. Politicians praise companies for acting "responsibly" or condemn them for not doing so. Yet the purpose of capitalism is to get great deals for consumers and investors. Corporate executives are not authorized by anyone—least of all by their investors—to balance profits against the public good. Nor do they have any expertise in making such moral calculations. Democracy is supposed to represent the public in drawing such lines. And the message that companies are moral beings with social responsibilities diverts public attention from the task of establishing such laws and rules in the first place.

It is much the same with what passes for corporate charity. Under today's intensely competitive form of global capitalism, companies donate money to good causes only to the extent the donation has public-relations value, thereby boosting the bottom line. But shareholders do not invest in firms expecting the money to be used for charitable purposes. They invest to earn high returns. Shareholders who wish to be charitable would, presumably, make donations to charities of their own choosing in amounts they decide for themselves. The larger danger is that these conspicuous displays of corporate beneficence hoodwink the public into believing corporations have charitable impulses that can be relied on in a pinch.

## Democracy Should Set the Rules

By pretending that the economic success corporations enjoy saddles them with particular social duties only serves to distract the public from democracy's responsibility to set the rules of the game and thereby protect the common good. The only way for the citizens in us to trump the consumers in us is through laws and rules that make our purchases and investments social choices as well as personal ones. A change in labor laws making it easier for employees to organize and negotiate better terms, for example, might increase the price of products and services. My inner consumer won't like that very much, but the citizen in me might think it a fair price to pay. A small transfer tax on sales of stock, to slow the movement of capital ever so slightly, might give communities a bit more time to adapt to changing circumstances. The return on my retirement fund might go down by a small fraction, but the citizen in me thinks it worth the price. Extended unemployment insurance combined with wage insurance and job training could ease the pain for workers caught in the downdrafts of globalization.

Let us be clear: The purpose of democracy is to accomplish ends we cannot achieve as individuals. But democracy cannot fulfill this role when companies use politics to advance or maintain their competitive standing, or when they appear to take on social responsibilities that they have no real capacity or authority to fulfill. That leaves societies unable to address the tradeoffs between economic growth and social problems such as job insecurity, widening inequality, and climate change. As a result, consumer and investor interests almost invariably trump common concerns.

The vast majority of us are global consumers and, at least indirectly, global investors. In these roles we should strive for the best deals possible. That is how we participate in the global market economy. But those private benefits usually have social costs. And for those of us living in democracies, it is imperative to remember that we are also citizens who have it in our power to reduce these social costs, making the true price of the goods and services we purchase as low as possible. We can accomplish this larger feat only if we take our roles as citizens seriously. The first step, which is often the hardest, is to get our thinking straight.

> "Though the regime always holds
> most of the power, insurrections
> that take advantage of the dynamics
> of information cascades thus offer
> protesters both offensive and defensive
> capabilities that they wouldn't
> otherwise have."

# The Internet Has Advanced Democratic Causes

*Clay Shirky*

*Clay Shirky studies the effects of the Internet on society and is the author of* Here Comes Everybody: The Power of Organizing Without Organizations. *In the following viewpoint, Shirky refutes criticism he received in the pages of* Prospect *magazine in 2009 for holding an "optimistic" view that social media helps unite resistance movements in non-democratic nations. Shirky defends this notion, claiming that the Internet has allowed disparate groups to coordinate collective protests against oppression and keep the world informed of abuses of power within troubled states. Shirky maintains that even if governments quell these resistance movements, they can never quite stop the flow of communication that will eventually bring more attention to fights for democratic reform.*

As you read, consider the following questions:

1. How do "information cascades" work, according to Shirky?

2. In the author's opinion, why did the protests in Belarus fail to stir popular discontent?

3. What Internet media site does Shirky say was flooded with hundreds of videos documenting the protests against the Iranian election outcomes?

In *Prospect*'s December [2009] cover story, "How Dictators Watch Us on the Web," Evgeny Morozov [a writer on the political impact of the Internet] criticises my views on the impact of social media on political unrest. Indeed, he even says I am "the man most responsible for the intellectual confusion over the political role of the internet." In part, I would like to agree with some of his criticisms, while partially disputing some of his assertions too.

Let me start with a basic statement of belief: because civic life is not just created by the actions of individuals, but by the actions of groups, the spread of mobile phones and internet connectivity will reshape that civic life, changing the ways members of the public interact with one another.

Though germane, this argument says little to nothing about the tempo, mode, or ultimate shape such a transformation will take. There are a number of possible scenarios for changed interaction between the public and the state, some rosy, others distinctly less so. Crucially however, Morozov's reading is in response to a specific strain of internet utopianism—let's call it the "just-add-internet" hypothesis. In this model, the effect of social media on the lives of citizens in authoritarian regimes will be swift, unstoppable, and positive—a kind of digitised 1989. And it will lead us to expect the prominence of social media in any society's rapid democratisation.

## Communications Media Can Encourage Political Participation

While this argument is overtly simplistic, I have nonetheless helped fuel it by discussing mechanisms through which citizens can coordinate group action, while failing to note the ways that visible public action also provides new counter-moves to repressive regimes. Morozov is right to criticise me for this imbalance, and for the resulting (and undue) optimism it engenders about social media as a democratising force; I stand corrected.

Nevertheless, I want to defend the notion—which Morozov goes after in the "man most responsible for intellectual confusion" section of his essay—that social media improves political information cascades, as outlined by the political scientist Susanne Lohmann. It also represents a new dynamic within political protest, which will alter the struggle between insurrectionists and the state, even if the state wins in any given clash. Where this will lead to a net advantage for popular uprisings in authoritarian regimes is an open question—and a point on which Morozov and I still disagree—but the new circumstances of coordinated public action, I believe, marks an essential change in the civilian part of the "arms race."

Lohmann's mechanism for how information cascades operate is simple: when a small group is willing to take public action against a regime, and the regime's reaction is muted, it provides information about the value of participation to the group of citizens who opted not to participate. Some members of this group will then join in the next round of protests.

In turn, further non-reaction by the regime will provide additional information to the next group of "fence-sitters," thereby increasing participation. Consequently, strong reaction by the regime can be effective in putting down insurrection, but at the same time risks constraining and, in extreme cases, delegitimising the regime itself. If the regime acts late, it can thus lose in one of two ways: the insurrections can win, or the state can win, but at Pyrrhic costs. Between those two cases, the state can also succeed in putting down the insurrection at low cost to itself.

Prior to the spread of social media, a typical classic case of late and failed reaction by the regime to an information cascade is the one documented by Lohmann, around the collapse of communism in eastern Europe. The classic case of late and successful reaction by a regime is Tiananmen Square and, even there, the subsequent alteration of the Chinese state continues to be driven in part by the recognition that without continued economic improvement, the same forces that drove insurrection might return. Though the regime always holds most of the power, insurrections that take advantage of the dynamics of information cascades thus offer protesters both offensive and defensive capabilities that they wouldn't otherwise have.

But both these examples took place prior to the invention of the internet and widespread use of mobile phones. The question, today, is what the increased ability on the part of citizens armed with those tools can do to achieve shared public knowledge and coordinated action.

## Resistance Organized Through Telecommunications

Morozov introduces both the Belarusian and Iranian protests as examples of places where this struggle can be seen. The October Square protests in Minsk in 2006 did not, however, destabilise the [Aleksandr] Lukashenko government, and surveillance of the mob on LiveJournal helped limit use of flash mob techniques by protesters. The flash mob participants were not able to use either the offensive or defensive capabilities of social media to permanent advantage—there is not enough discontent in the rest of the population to cause them to join in, the government's reaction was sufficiently swift and harsh, and documentation of those events did not resonate outside the country.

Sadly for residents of Belarus, leaders of countries with low geopolitical importance will always find it easier to deflect demo-

## Mobile Phones Aid the Spread of Information and Support Democracy

Social capital and a lively public sphere are key components of a democracy. The increasing flow of information through mobile devices extends the public sphere. Mobile phones have enlarged the amount of information available and at the same time reduced the role of gatekeepers. . . . Similarly, mobile phones open private spaces in countries where politics is controlled by the government. With the growing proliferation of handsets and the increase in their use, the source and diffusion of calls and text messages become more difficult to control (in contrast to the Internet). North Korea, for example, tries to ban mobile phones altogether to avoid unmediated contact and information exchange beyond the state's control. Mobile phones are credited with creating greater transparency in elections, for example in Zambia (2001) and Kenya (2002) as election observers were able to disseminate results directly to central authorities, eliminating opportunities for election rigging in the transmission process.

*Heike Hermanns, "Mobile Democracy:*
*Mobile Phones as Democratic Tools," Politics,*
*vol. 28, no. 2 2008.*

cratic movements, social media or no, than leaders in more strategically vital countries. The case of Belarus is therefore one in which protesters have been given new capabilities for organising, but where the state's reaction has remained effective. In the arms race in Minsk, the tools have changed, but the end result resembles the old equilibrium state. This is the kind of outcome whose strategic ramifications Morozov has highlighted better than anyone.

The Iranian situation, which Morozov also mentions, is much more complex: the government relies more on its perceived legitimacy, both democratic and theocratic, than Belarus. Moreover, Iran's geopolitical importance is paramount on many fronts at once. Clearly, the protests following the 12th June [2009] elections were aided by social media. Although Twitter got top billing in western accounts, the most important tools during the Tehran protests were mobile phones, whether to send text messages, photos, or videos. Twitter, predominantly, was a gateway to Western attention.

By the time the regime managed to shut down the various modes of communication available to the Tehran protesters, they were retiring to rooftops and shouting slogans into the night. Although this act of coordination did not use technology per se, it was made possible by the visible evidence provided by users documenting and broadcasting the earlier solidarity of the street protests. This is why figures showing how few people use social media for political change are red herrings.

Insurrections, even pro-democracy insurrections, always begin as minority affairs, driven by a small, young, and well-educated population before they expand more widely. In the Iranian case, once the information about general discontent had successfully cascaded, the coordination among the populace remained intact, even when the tools which helped disseminate that information were shut down.

## Regimes Cannot Shut Communications Down Indefinitely

This makes the situation in Tehran a key test. As usual, the state has more power than the insurgents, but the insurgency has nevertheless achieved the transition from distributed but uncoordinated discontent to being an actual protest movement, and part of that transition was achieved with these tools. [Mir-Hossein] Mousavi [a reform candidate in the 2009 election], and other opposition figures, now know that when they speak out, they do so representing a public, rather than an aggregate of discontented individuals. And when mass action does become possible, it again unleashes protests, as seen in the incredible outpouring of anti-Khamenei [the religious leader of Iran] sentiment on 13 Aban (4th November), usually a day of anti-American protest—an outpouring documented hundreds of times via videos posted to YouTube.

It is impossible to know how the next few months in Iran will unfold, but the use of social media has already passed several tests: it has enabled citizens to coordinate with one another better than previously, to broadcast events like Basij violence or the killing of Neda Aga Soltan [a bystander shot during June 2009 protests in Iran] to the rest of the world, and, by forcing the regime to shut down communications apparatus, the protesters have infected Iran with a kind of technological auto-immune disease. However great the regime's short-term desire to keep the protesters from communicating with one another, a modern economy simply cannot function if people can't use their phones. The regime may yet crush protests, but even if they do, the events of June to November this year will still have broken the old illusion of a happy balance between democratic, theocratic, and military power in Iran.

I accept Morozov's criticism of *Here Comes Everybody* [Shirky's 2008 book about the organizing power of social media]. That book was about social media rather than politics—it was an imbalanced account of the arms race between citizens and their governments. However, even within the logic of the arms race, the easier the assembly of citizens, the more ubiquitous the ability to document atrocities. And the more the self-damaging measures which states take—like shutting down mobile phones networks—will resolve themselves as a net advantage for insurrection within authoritarian regimes. Net advantage, in some cases, is a far cry from the "just-add-internet" hypothesis, but it is a view that is considerably more optimistic about the balance of power between citizens and the state than Morozov's.

> "It turns out that Twitter-based activism is easily managed in a country where the government has near-total control over Internet access."

# The Internet Has Not Advanced Democratic Causes

### Hiawatha Bray

*In the viewpoint that follows,* Boston Globe *technology reporter Hiawatha Bray contends that the Internet and other communications media can bring like-minded political activists together in unfree nations, but these social media do not breed or spread democracy. Citing the work of author and political scholar Evgeny Morozov, Bray points out how revolutions amplified by Twitter and the Internet have still been crushed by totalitarian regimes. Worse, these regimes have learned how to manipulate the Internet to spread their own propaganda and track dissidents, Bray remarks. Ultimately Bray worries that building dissent on the Internet is not the same as taking revolution to the streets, and he maintains that no despotic governments have been overthrown by people sitting in front of computer screens.*

As you read, consider the following questions:

1. As Bray writes, how have autocratic governments employed the Internet as a "safety valve"?

2. According to the author, who, besides government ministers, is helping keep government propaganda circulating on the Internet?

3. In Bray's view, why is the fact that everyone is equal on the Internet a problem for fomenting revolution in unfree countries?

I sn't Iran supposed to be a free country by now?

Less than two years ago [in 2009], tens of thousands of angry citizens filled the streets of Tehran, denouncing the country's fraudulent elections. These protesters had the fervent support of millions in America and Europe.

Better yet, they had Internet services like Twitter and Facebook, which helped them organize rallies and beamed images of their struggle to an outraged world.

Armed with youth, vigor, and the power of the Internet, how could these protesters lose? But lose they did, and decisively.

It turns out that Twitter-based activism is easily managed in a country where the government has near-total control over Internet access. Indeed, Iranian leaders soon realized that the Internet could be a despot's best friend. They created blogs to spew pro-government propaganda and learned to scour social networking sites as an easy way to track the regime's opponents, and their online friends as well.

## Misplaced Faith in the Twitter Revolution

The crushing of Iran's Twitter Revolution has come as a severe disappointment to liberal citizens of the West. We've been bred to the idea that ever-greater access to information inevitably leads to the spread of freedom and democracy. But in his sardonic,

## Thailand's Crackdown on Political Dissent

Some governments are combining aggressive Internet laws with truly innovative measures aimed at identifying and barring undesired content early on in the publishing cycle. The Thai government, for example, uses the country's severe *lèse majesté* laws, prohibiting any offensive material aimed at the reigning sovereign, to go after administrators of critical Web sites. The most recent case is that of Cheeranuch Premchaiphorn, the Web administrator of Prachatai, the most influential Thai political Web site, who was recently detained [in March 2009] because a comment critical of the king was discovered on the site. The Thai authorities also "crowdsource" the process of gathering URLs of sites to be blocked by encouraging their loyalists to submit such sites for review (a site named ProtectTheKing.net is a primary collection point of the offensive URLs). Predictably, it's a one-way street: there is no similar invitation to submit sites to unblock.

*Evgeny Morozov, "The Internet: A Room of Our Own?," Dissent, Summer 2009.*

powerful new book, "The Net Delusion," Evgeny Morozov rips this idea to shreds. He shows how the world's autocrats have learned to love the Internet. Nations like Iran, China, and Venezuela now embrace it as a tool of propaganda and public surveillance. They've even learned to use the Internet as a social safety valve, where disgruntled citizens can blow off steam without posing a serious threat to the establishment.

Meanwhile, many Westerners cling to a simplistic fantasy that truth alone will set people free. Morozov thinks it's because we learned the wrong lesson from the fall of the old Soviet Union, a brittle old dictatorship that was terrified by the free flow of information. Histories of the Cold War often note that the spread of technologies like the videocassette player and the photocopier exposed many Soviet citizens to Western news and entertainment, and their images of freedom and prosperity.

These works often suggest that information technology played a major role in the Soviet collapse.

But as Morozov notes, that decline had far more to do with a decaying economy and an elite no longer willing to commit mass murder to stay in power. Western media played a marginal role at best. He even cites research showing that residents of communist East Germany who could pick up West German TV broadcasts actually became less likely to rebel; they were too busy watching "Dallas," "Dynasty," and "Miami Vice."

## The Tyrants Learn to Control the Power of the Internet

Today's dictators get it. Internet users in countries like China may search in vain for information about the Tiananmen massacre [in 1989], but they can get all the Western movies and TV shows they want. In addition, China and other unfree countries have developed their own Internet institutions, including search engines, social networks, and even alternatives to the online reference site Wikipedia.

Written in the national language and tailored to the specific culture, these sites are often far more popular than their Western counterparts. Of course, these sites are careful to follow the official government line. Dissenting ideas are gently airbrushed away.

And don't suppose that pro-regime materials are cranked out solely by some bureaucrat at the Ministry of Truth. Plenty of patriotic Chinese or Iranian bloggers will stand up for their country without any prodding.

Controlling governments have learned to recruit these loyal citizens for their online propaganda campaigns.

Meanwhile, we Westerners continue to harbor illusions about the power of online organizing. But such Internet activism can provide governments with new tools of control. "The new technologies allow us to identify conspirators and those who are violating the law, without having to control all people individually," Iran's police chief said early last year amid concerns about possible renewed unrest over the disputed elections.

Online political sites are also tempting targets for government-backed hacking. Morozov tells of how Vietnam hacked into the website of a well-known refugee organization and planted a virus there.

Anybody who downloaded software from the site got a little something extra—a program that let Vietnamese authorities track their online activities.

## The Failures of Armchair Activism

But an excessive reliance on cyber-activism poses a subtler danger. It threatens to turn revolutionary movements into mere salons of fiery political conversation. Amid all the tweets and status updates of the Iranian uprising, few were engaged in the hard, dangerous, face-to-face business of building a real political movement. Everybody's equal on the Internet, but a revolution needs leaders, and Twitter isn't very good at producing them. Online organizing has its uses, Morozov says. But apart from traditional grass-roots activism, it's little more than a nuisance to the people in power.

Morozov wants American foreign policy to encourage the spread of democracy, and agrees that there's a role for the Internet. But he rightly insists on a top-to-bottom rethink of that role.

Apart from a few sensible suggestions on the book's final two pages, Morozov leaves this vital task to others.

It's too bad that so trenchant an analyst has so few positive prescriptions to offer. Still, Morozov has produced an invaluable book. Copies should be smuggled to every would-be Twitter revolutionary, and to their clueless groupies in the Western democracies.

# Periodical Bibliography

*The following articles have been selected to supplement the diverse views presented in this chapter.*

| | |
|---|---|
| James Allan | "Intimations of the Decline of Democracy," *Quadrant*, May 2010. |
| Peter Beinart | "Is Freedom Failing?," *Time*, May 21, 2007. |
| Ian Bremmer | "Democracy in Cyberspace," *Foreign Affairs*, November/December 2010. |
| Tom de Luca and John Buell | "Free Trade: A Paradox for Democracy," *New Political Science*, December 2006. |
| Daniel Deudney and G. John Ikenberry | "The Myth of the Autocratic Revival: Why Liberal Democracy Will Prevail," *Foreign Affairs*, January/February 2009. |
| Jaap de Wilde | "The Mirage of Global Democracy," *European Review*, February 2011. |
| Michael Goodhart | "Human Rights and Global Democracy," *Ethics and International Affairs*, 2008. |
| Robin Hahnel | "Why the Market Subverts Democracy," *American Behavioral Scientist*, March 2009. |
| Jason McLure | "Africa's Failing Democracies," *Newsweek*, July 12, 2010. |
| Evgeny Morozov | "The Internet: A Room of Our Own?," *Dissent*, Summer 2009. |
| Eli M. Noam | "Why the Internet Is Bad for Democracy," *Communications of the ACM*, October 2005. |
| Mark F. Plattner | "Populism, Pluralism, and Liberal Democracy," *Journal of Democracy*, January 2010. |

OPPOSING
VIEWPOINTS®
SERIES

# Can There Be Democracy in the Middle East?

# Chapter Preface

In an October 21, 2002, article for the *Weekly Standard*, Victor Davis Hanson, a professor of military history, set forth his fears concerning the expected US military invasion of Iraq because of that country's supposed possession of weapons of mass destruction. With war looming, Hanson questioned the United States' plans for Iraq after what he assumed would be a US victory. Hanson heard the boasts of overthrowing the Iraqi dictator Saddam Hussein and bringing democracy to the land, but he was unsure if post-war Iraq could become democratic. "Iraq is a Muslim country," he wrote, "with no tradition of consensual government or even an indigenous vocabulary for 'democracy,' 'citizen,' 'secularism,' or 'referendum.' The realists remind us that the seeds of constitutional government do not grow in soil that lacks a middle class and the rule of law. They point out that there has never been a truly free Arab democracy in 1,500 years." Hanson worried that the government's pledge of democracy promotion might devolve simply in setting up another "pro-American despotism like Saudi Arabia and Egypt" that would pay lip service to liberal reforms but continue to oppress the population while enriching itself on oil reserves to sell to its new Western allies.

After the defeat of Hussein's forces in 2003, other observers adopted the skepticism espoused by critics like Hanson before the war. In an April 20, 2003, editorial for *Prospect* magazine, Adam Garfinkle, the editor of the *American Interest*, warned against any attempt by the George W. Bush administration to impose a blanket democratization strategy on newly-liberated Iraq. Garfinkle claimed, "If the administration does proceed with a broad and rapid democratisation, it is likely to produce the worst possible result: failing to produce Arab democracy, yet reaping untold resentment for trying." Garfinkle based his criticism on his conviction that "in different degrees, Arab societies lack three prerequisites for democracy: the belief that the source of political authority is intrinsic to society; a concept of majority rule; and the acceptance of all citizens' equality before the law." He maintains that democracy might take hold in Arab countries in the future, but the desire for the rule of law must come from within these nations and not be imposed from outside.

Garfinkle's concerns, however, over forthcoming disaster did not materialize after the country held national elections in 2005 to form a coalition parliament made up of Shia and Sunni Muslims as well as the Kurdish minority that inhabits the mountainous northern border. Four years later, when new elections were held, the *Wall Street Journal* posted a November 10 editorial praising the determination of the government and the people to keep democratic reform on track. The newspaper noted that the 2009 elections were the first "open" elections in the post-war climate, allowing Iraqis to vote for any candidate that chose to run for office. "The immediate result from the switch to open lists will be to reduce the power and attraction of sectarian parties and enlarge the political field. Iraqis will have a greater choice," the editorial stated.

Whether Iraq will become a shining example of grassroots democracy in the Middle East is yet to be determined. However, in more recent times, anti-authoritarian demonstrations have sprung up in other Arab nations, leading many to believe that the trend toward popular and just rule may be the first steps toward democracy in the region. The authors in the following chapter explore the possibility of a democratic movement taking hold in the Middle East.

> *"Most Arab Muslims have neither embraced nor installed what they have long regarded as an irreligious and even pagan ideology—secular democracy."*

# Western Democracy Will Never Take Hold in the Middle East

*Michael Scheuer*

*A former official with the CIA, Michael Scheuer is currently a professor of security studies at Georgetown University in Washington, DC. Scheuer asserts in the following viewpoint that while many Arab nations are modernizing, they are not becoming more secular. Scheuer contends that Western powers are incorrect to assume that modernization will lead to secular democracy in the Arab world. According to Scheuer, Arabs largely support government founded on strict Islamic code, and they consider Western secularization a threat to their religious identity. For this reason, Scheuer insists Westerners must rethink their policy toward Arab countries and stop incurring the ire of Islamic peoples by trying to seduce them with Western culture and liberal democracy.*

Michael Scheuer, "Illiberal Islam," *American Conservative*, vol. 10, no. 5, May, 2011. All rights reserved. Reproduced by permission.

As you read, consider the following questions:

1. Why does Scheuer claim that Islamist groups have such a strong influence on Arab societies?

2. How are Islamists using technological innovation against Western aggressors, according to Scheuer?

3. As Scheuer writes, during the ongoing war in Afghanistan, what secular trappings did the West import to Kabul that angered the Afghan people?

The Arab world's unrest has brought forth gushing, rather adolescent analysis about what the region will look like a year or more hence. Americans have decided that these upheavals have everything to do with the advent of liberalism, secularism, and Westernization in the region and that Islamist militant groups like al-Qaeda have been sidelined by the historically inevitable triumph of democracy—a belief that sounds a bit like the old Marxist-Leninist claptrap about iron laws of history and communism's inexorable triumph.

How has this judgment been reached? Primarily by disregarding facts, logic, and history, and instead relying on (a) the thin veneer of young, educated, pro-democracy, and English-speaking Muslims who can be found on Facebook and Twitter and (b) the employees of the BBC, CNN, and most other media networks, who have suspended genuine journalism in favor of cheerleading for secularism and democracy on the basis of a non-representative sample of English-speaking street demonstrators and users of social-networking sites. The West's assessment of Arab unrest so far has been—to paraphrase [fictional detective] Sam Spade's comment about the Maltese Falcon—the stuff that dreams, not reality, are made of.

## The Powerful Pull of Islam

A year from now [in 2012], we will find that most Arab Muslims have neither embraced nor installed what they have long regarded as an irreligious and even pagan ideology—secular democracy. They will have instead adhered even more closely to the faith that has graced, ordered, and regulated their lives for more than 1400 years, and which helped them endure the oppressive rule of Western-supported tyrants and kleptocrats.

This does not mean that fanatically religious regimes will dominate the region, but a seven-year Gallup survey of the Muslim world published in 2007 shows that a greater degree of Sharia law in governance is favored by young and old, moderates and militants, men and even women in most Muslim countries. While a façade of democracy may well appear in new regimes in places like Egypt and Tunisia, their governments will be heavily influenced by the military and by Islamist organizations like the Muslim Brotherhood and al-Qaeda. If for no other reason, the Islamist groups will have a powerful pull because they have strong organizational capabilities; wide allegiance among the highly educated in the military, hard sciences, engineering, religious faculties, and medicine; and a reservoir of patience for a two-steps-forward, one-step-back strategy that is beyond Western comprehension. We in the West too often forget, for example, that the Muslim Brotherhood and al-Qaeda draw from Muslim society's best and brightest, not its dregs; that al-Qaeda has been waging its struggle for 25 years, the Muslim Brotherhood for nearly 85 years; and that Islam has been in the process of globalizing since the 7th century.

As new Arab regimes develop, Westerners also are likely to find that their own deep sense of superiority over devout Muslims—which is especially strong among the secular left, Christian evangelicals, and neoconservatives—is unwarranted. The nearly universal assumption in the West is that Islamic governance could not possibly satisfy the aspirations of Muslims for greater freedom and increased economic opportunity—this even though Iran has a more representative political system than that of any state in the region presided over by a Western-backed dictator. No regime run by the Muslim Brotherhood would look like Canada, but it would be significantly less oppressive than those run by the al-Sauds [the ruling family of Saudi Arabia] and [former Egyptian President Hosni] Mubarak. This is not to say it would be similar to or more friendly toward the West—neither will be the case—but in terms of respecting and addressing basic human concerns they will be less monstrous.

## Modernization Without Secularization

The West's biggest surprise a year out may well lie in being forced to learn that Westernization, secularization, and modernization are not synonyms. The postwar West's arrogance—dare I say hubris?—has long held as an article of its increasingly pagan faith that these concepts are identical, inseparable, and the proudest achievement of superior Western culture. Well, not so. Muslims make an absolute distinction among the concepts.

Modernization, in the sense of the tools of technology, is something they pursue with a passion. From air-conditioning to computers to a variety of other communications gear and high-tech weaponry, there is little Luddism [an antipathy toward technology] among Muslims. Indeed, the military forces of the United States are now losing wars to Islamist *mujahideen* who stay one step ahead of Western military technology in areas like improvised explosive devices and using topography to disguise their locations from satellite photography. Through their sophisticated use of the Internet and other media vehicles, moreover, they are dominating the so-called information war and making Western propaganda efforts appear for what they are: reality-defying, intellectually sterile, and designed for the non-existent I-am-ready-to-blow-myself-up-because-Americans-drink-beer Islamist enemy.

As Washington and its allies remain locked in two wars with Islamists—and itch to start another in Libya—they are cultivating a new generation of Muslim enemies by neglecting the fundamental difference, for Muslims and other non-Westerners, between modernization on one hand and Westernization and secularization on the other. In Steve Coll's fine book, *The Bin Ladens*, he describes the late Saudi King Faisal as a champion of technical progress without privatization of religion; indeed, Faisal was an austere and pious man who was the motive force behind an attempt to modernize the kingdom, but at the same time he was prepared to resist secularism with force. As Coll also notes, Osama bin Laden attended a "modern" school that taught math, sciences, geography, and English—as well as faith—that was established by Faisal. Bin Laden, Coll writes, received an up-to-date but fiercely anti-secular education that was "inseparable from the national ideology promoted by King Faisal in the late years of his reign."

This is the point at which the West's jejune expectations for secular democracy in the Muslim world will come dramatically a cropper in the years ahead. By willfully misinterpreting English-speaking, pro-democracy Egyptian, Libyan, and Tunisian Facebookers as representing the Arab world's welcoming view of secularism, Western leaders, especially the media, have deluded one another into believing that Islam's doors are open for women's rights, pornography, blasphemy, man-made law, popular elections, and a host of the West's other secular-pagan attributes.

In this judgment they will be dead wrong, and they will find that any Western help dispatched to move Muslim societies in these directions will earn the Faisal/bin Laden response: fierce and possibly violent resistance. Two examples of this phenomenon—one country specific, one international—are already on display.

## Backlash Against Western Secularizing

In Afghanistan, the country's post-2001 inundation by Western non-governmental organizations and private-sector construction, mercenary, and consulting firms brought with it bars, bordellos, and the proliferation of Western dress—all viewed by many pious Afghan Muslims as offenses to their faith. The creation of this pint-sized version of Hollywood's lifestyle in Kabul had particularly unfortunate consequences for the U.S.-led coalition. This un-Islamic behavior helped prompt much of the city's citizenry to collect and pass information about the West's military and civil plans—and those of the [Hamid] Karzai regime that abetted the Westerners—to the Taliban and other *mujahideen* groups for violent exploitation.

Worldwide, the West's extravagant—not to say mindless—praise for the once Muslim but now anti-Islamic feminist Ayaan Hirsi Ali is a further example of its ignorance about the depth of anti-secularism in the Muslim world. Hirsi Ali is the perfect embodiment of the West's unshakeable conviction—best expressed by Secretary [of State Hillary] Clinton and [former Secretary of State] Madeleine Albright—that Muslim women want to be "just like us." This Western image of Hirsi Ali as a kind of Joan of Arc bent on freeing Muslim women from their religion's superstitious shackles is shared by some Muslim women—but very few. The bulk of reliable polling data by Gallup shows most Muslim men and women alike want a large measure of Sharia law to be employed by the regimes that govern them. There is no data showing that Muslim women long to decamp to a semi-pagan society where Lady Gaga and Lindsay Lohan are role models.

Indeed, the West's heroic Hirsi Ali tends to be viewed in the Islamic world as an apostate to her faith. She also is seen as a new edition of the British imperialist Lord Curzon, bent on performing anew [author Rudyard] Kipling's call for improving the lot of her little brown sisters by *diktat* or force.

At day's end, the success of the United States and its allies in concluding their war with the Islamist movement depends on an adult assessment of the Muslim world. The basis of this analysis must be a realization that modernization, Westernization, and secularization are not interchangeable terms. The technological tools of the West are largely welcomed, admired, and used in the Muslim world—witness the wars in Iraq and Afghanistan—but continuing attempts to impose

Westernization and privatization of religion will, at this point in history, remain a vibrant *casus belli* [justification for war] for Muslims and earn a fierce and martial resistance.

We must begin to recognize that while America's neoconservative and progressive thinkers fallaciously prattle on about the Islamists being on the verge of Islamicizing the West, it is the West's half-century campaign to impose and then maintain secularist tyrants on Muslim states that has supplied the main motivation for the growing number of Muslims who believe themselves and their faith to be at war against the West. Continued failure to make this simple and clear semantic distinction will bring the late Professor [Samuel] Huntington's concept of a clash of civilizations much closer to fruition.

| "Liberal democracy grows only in
certain cultures."

# Islam Remains a Barrier to Democracy in the Middle East

*Whitson G. Waldo III*

*In the following viewpoint, Whitson G. Waldo III contends that Islamic law, or Shari'a, is incompatible with democracy, and therefore the Middle East will likely remain in the grip of theocratic regimes. According to Waldo, Shari'a, unlike democracy, does not hold everyone equal before the law, nor does it brook any form of dissent. In fact, Waldo asserts that dissension is punished swiftly and brutally, effectively discouraging most Muslims from speaking out in favor of liberal reforms. Because so many of those living in Islamic nations view the state and religion as identical, it is unlikely, Waldo argues, that these lands will ever embrace democracy, despite protests against reigning governments. Whitson G. Waldo III is currently a rancher; he has also worked extensively in the semiconductor industry.*

As you read, consider the following questions:

1. In Waldo's view, how has Turkey recently begun backsliding away from the secular, democratic tendencies the

government adopted after World War I?

2. According to Waldo, who presides over trials in nations ruled by Shari'a?

3. As the author states, why are there no Christian churches in Saudi Arabia?

The world has been mesmerized by the uprisings taking place [in 2011] in the Middle East against authoritarian regimes. Some speculation is that this effect was caused by the example of Iraq sustaining multiple democratic cycles. By force, the [George W.] Bush administration annihilated Saddam [Hussein's] brutal regime and forced into place a democratic process. The speculation is that people in neighboring countries have been observant of the changes and now seek democracy for themselves. However, a liberal democracy is comprised of particular attributes such as representative government, rule of law, equality before the law, just punishment, property rights, and certain freedoms (e.g., religion, speech, association, etc.). It remains to be seen what the Iraqis and, for that matter, the rest of the Middle Eastern revolutionaries make of their opportunity.

Liberal democracy grows only in certain cultures. History has empirically demonstrated that cultures stemming from Christian, Eastern, and Far Eastern religions are compatible with stable, long term liberal democracies. On the other hand, it is not obvious that cultures emanating from an Islamic foundation are compatible with liberal democracy. This uncertainty is a key reason the European Union has resisted integrating Turkey. It may explain why there are no Muslim liberal democracies.

## Shari'a Is Opposed to Liberal Reform

After World War I, Mustafa Ataturk brought the power of the Turkish state to bear against fundamentalist Islam. In an attempt to modernize, Ataturk forcibly introduced Western systems and required a secular bent. However, in current times, Recep

Erdogan has leveraged public disapproval of government corruption, incompetence, and ineffectiveness to make gains in legislative representation. His Justice and Development Party, with ties to an earlier Islamist party, have been leading Turkey since 2002. While shari'a has not been formally declared the law of the land, a cultural shift is apparent by observing the effects of increased pressure on women to conform to Islamic dress styles (e.g., head scarves, veils) and public behaviors (fewer single women about, fewer women intermingling with men socially, etc.). In a downward trend, Freedom House notes the loss of freedoms of speech and the press. Even Turkey's president, Abdullah Gul, admits civil liberties are endangered. Within the last year, in foreign affairs, Turkey has distanced itself from Israel and moved closer to Syria, a client state of Iran. Also, Turkey instigated the attempt to break Israel's blockade of Gaza in order to aid the Muslim Brotherhood progeny Hamas. The Muslim Brotherhood aims to install totalitarian Islamist governments in all Muslim countries; oppression and persecution of non-believers is conjoined with their goals and not incidental.

New constitutions for both Afghanistan and Iraq were catalyzed by the United States. Unfortunately, both of their constitutions include diametrically opposed ideas. For example, both constitutions convey freedom of religion to citizens. But both also recognize the supremacy of Islamic law known as shari'a. Shari'a is opposed to freedom of religion. This tension suggests shari'a or the constitution must give. So far, in both countries, illiberal shari'a has prevailed. On several occasions, Afghanistan has attempted to impose the shari'a penalty of death on Afghans who converted to Christianity from Islam. And Iraq's Christian population has been targeted for violence to the extent that a small fraction of believers remain in their country today compared to several years ago.

Iran purports to be a democracy. But the current repression against the Green Movement after the corrupted 2009 presidential election indicates little tolerance for dissent against the

## The Middle Ages and the Middle East

Judaism and Christianity have learned to come to terms with their marginalization in the public square. But to Muslims offended by a mere cartoon, that detachment or tolerance simply means that Judaism and Christianity have been emasculated. The Islamic world is, in short, as theocentric as the West was during its own fourteenth century, a time of the powerful emperors and popes, of crusades (aka jihad) and inquisitions. And democracy is as unlikely to succeed in the Middle East as it would have in the Middle Ages.

*Manfred Weidhorn, "Islam's Presumed Superiority to the West,"* Midwest Quarterly, *Autumn 2007.*

theocracy. Following the fall in 1979 of Mohammad Reza Shah Pahlavi by the Iranian Revolution, Khomeinists [followers of the Ayatollah Khomeini] established a theocratic constitution. This has prevented any effective liberal opposition from forming legally. Now, that opposition is being brutally repressed even to the point of civilian deaths.

## One State, One Religion

It is difficult to establish causality for the reason Muslim countries are inhospitable to liberal democracies. But there are many reasons shari'a is incompatible with classical liberalism. A leading reason is that shari'a is a totalitarian system brooking no dissent. Submission is required by shari'a of believers and non-believers alike. There is no quarter given for debate or reasoning.

One feature of liberal democracy is representative government. Juxtaposed against this is shari'a's imposition of poll taxes on non-believers in order to discourage participation. Also, there can be prohibitions against non-believers holding government office or judicial positions. Shari'a does not recognize the separation of mosque and state, so only particular political parties are allowed to form.

The rule of law is central to liberal democracy. However, shari'a doesn't consist of codified statutes per se. Rather, shari'a includes Koranic content and practices of Mohammed (sunna). Any fatwa, or religious ruling, issued by innumerable individuals, could result in an ex post facto hazard. Also, there are no trials by jury, but only trials before religious officials.

Equality before the law means that men and women have equal legal standing in a liberal democracy. But shari'a devalues the worth of women. As witnesses, a woman has half the value of a man. This means two women must contest one man's claims. A wife must prove her innocence if a husband accuses her of adultery, but a wife must prove her husband's guilt if she accuses. Wife beating is the prerogative of her husband's governance. Females are entitled to half the inheritance of males. Also, drawing the greatest distinction in inequality, shari'a countenances slavery. Enslavement can range from servitude to treatment as chattel (i.e., the slave does not retain even rights over his/her own body).

## Punishment for Dissent

Liberal democracies eschew cruel and unusual punishments. But shari'a requires imprisonment and even severing of a hand of a thief, stoning to death for adultery by married men or women, and lashings for other sexual transgressions. Homosexual behavior and sodomy are punishable by death.

Property rights are not uniform under shari'a. For example, Saudi Arabia has no churches anywhere in the country. Elsewhere, in Muslim countries, it is not uncommon that

Christians may not build churches. For churches that already exist, approval might be withheld to effect repairs.

Shari'a does not sanction freedom of speech or the press. The orchestrated worldwide violence protesting the [Danish newspaper] *Jyllands-Posten* cartoons of September 30, 2005 depicting Mohammed is consistent with Islamic fundamentalism. Contesting Islamic beliefs is considered heresy and punishable by death. This is consistent with the lack of freedom of religion imposed by shari'a. Apostasy is a capital offense. The Koran encourages conversion at the point of the sword and permits killing non-believers who won't convert.

Optimists, multiculturalists, ignoramuses, and naifs think protesters in the Middle East will replace tyrannies with liberal democracies. Unfortunately, you can't get to there from where the protesters are starting. With the sole exception of Israel, cultures in the Middle East, dominated as they are by shari'a, are inimical to liberal democracy and liberty. Tyrants may fall, but any democracies that are established will devolve sooner or later into the totalitarian state that shari'a demands. In general, American foreign policy decisions should be informed by the constraints shari'a imposes on movement into modernity in the Middle East. In particular, Americans should not expend one drop of blood or any treasure on current or future uprisings in the Middle East.

*"[The Muslim Brotherhood] is
committed to imposing Islamic law
(Sharia), which would severely restrict
the freedoms of Egyptians."*

# The Muslim Brotherhood Is a Threat to Democratic Change in Egypt

*James Phillips*

*James Phillips is a senior research fellow for Middle Eastern affairs
at the Heritage Foundation, a conservative, public policy think
tank. In the following viewpoint, he warns that the Muslim Brotherhood is a dangerous Islamist organization that seeks to subvert
liberal reform in Egypt. According to Phillips, the Muslim Brotherhood is determined to hijack the reform process in the wake of
the downfall of President Hosni Mubarak's oppressive regime and
turn Egypt into a strict Islamic nation that would curtail freedoms
enjoyed by the citizenry. Phillips insists the United States should
refrain from intervening in the reform process so as not to win the
Brotherhood more support among Egyptians who might interpret
such American interference as imperialistic.*

James Phillips, "Egypt's Muslim Brotherhood Lurks as a Long-Term Threat to Freedom,"
*Heritage Foundation WebMemo #3138*, February 8, 2011. Used by permission of Heritage
Foundation.

As you read, consider the following questions:

1. Who is Mohamed ElBaradei, as the author describes him?
2. Why does Phillips claim the Muslim Brotherhood currently holds an advantage over secular reform parties in Egypt?
3. What two sectors of the Egyptian population does Phillips believe will suffer unduly if Egypt adopts Sharia, or Islamic law?

Although Egypt's widely supported protest movement was reportedly instigated by secular opposition activists, the largest and most well-organized group within Egypt's diverse coalition of opposition groups remains the Muslim Brotherhood, an Islamist movement determined to transform Egypt into an Islamic state that is hostile to freedom. The Muslim Brotherhood has joined other opposition groups in negotiating with Vice President Omar Suleiman over the ground rules for establishing a transitional government.

In facilitating a transition to a more representative government, the [Barack] Obama Administration should be careful that it does not also inadvertently help the Muslim Brotherhood advance its anti-freedom agenda.

## A History of Hatred

The Muslim Brotherhood, founded in 1928, is the Middle East's oldest and most influential Islamist movement. Outlawed in Egypt since 1954, when it attempted to assassinate former President Gamal Abdel Nasser, the Brotherhood has seen its leaders repeatedly jailed and has been forced to moderate its violent proclivities. Although it has changed its tactics, it retains the long-term goal of creating an Islamist state that would be an enemy of freedom.

An offshoot of the Brotherhood, Egyptian Islamic Jihad, assassinated President Anwar Sadat in 1981, perpetrated a series of

Muslim Brotherhood; Cartoon by BART, www.CartoonStock.com.; BART Reproduction rights obtainable from www.CartoonStock.com.

terrorist attacks in Egypt in the 1990s, and became part of [the terrorist organization] al-Qaeda. Another offshoot, the Palestinian Islamist extremist group Hamas, won elections in Gaza in 2006, staged a coup in 2007 to transform Gaza into a terrorist base, and remains committed to destroying Israel.

The Muslim Brotherhood's strategy is to lie low in the current crisis and work behind the secular gadfly Mohamed ElBaradei, a spokesman for the broad opposition coalition who is far better known outside of Egypt than inside the country. The former U.N. bureaucrat is a lackluster political novice who commands little grassroots support and would be a useful figurehead to defuse Western anxiety while the Brotherhood organizes behind the scenes to transform the disjointed popular revolt into a draconian Islamist revolution.

The populist revolt now has broad-based popular support from a wide spectrum of political movements, but so did the French, Russian, and Iranian revolutions in their early stages before well-organized revolutionary minorities ruthlessly established dominance and erected dictatorships to enforce their antidemocratic ideologies.

## The Dangers the Brotherhood Poses

The Muslim Brotherhood has a clear advantage over Egypt's weak and fractured secular opposition parties because it has enjoyed a head start in organizing politically. The [Hosni] Mubarak regime crushed the secular opposition while allowing the Muslim Brotherhood to operate just enough to scare the U.S. and other Western nations into buying its line that only Mubarak stood between the Islamists and power. Brotherhood candidates were allowed to run as independents in the 2005 elections and won about 20 percent of the seats in Egypt's parliament. In contrast, the secular parties are poorly financed and badly organized and, because of systematic government repression, have had little opportunity to build a popular base.

If it comes to power, the Muslim Brotherhood will inevitably be hostile to the values and interests of the United States. It is committed to imposing Islamic law (Sharia), which would severely restrict the freedoms of Egyptians, particularly women and the Christian minority, which comprises about 10 percent of Egypt's population. It insists that only a Muslim male can lead the nation. The Brotherhood's Islamist ideology will lead it to renege on Egypt's current commitment to fight Islamist terrorism and possibly its nonproliferation obligations. It is sure to undermine and eventually abrogate Egypt's 1979 peace treaty with Israel and work with its junior partner Hamas to plunge the region into a series of crises and wars that will threaten Egypt, Israel, the Palestinians, and Jordan, which also has a peace treaty with Israel.

Ultimately, an Egypt dominated by the Muslim Brotherhood would further destabilize an already volatile region and deal a disastrous blow to American power and influence in the Middle East.

## Keep the Muslim Brotherhood at Arm's Length

To limit the Muslim Brotherhood's ability to undermine both Egypt's freedoms and America's interests in the region, the Obama Administration should keep it at arm's length. Embracing the Brotherhood would only demoralize pro-Western opposition movements and lead them to accommodate themselves to its rising power. Rather than inserting itself into the delicate negotiations over the transition to a new government, Washington should allow the Egyptian military establishment—the only institution in Egypt capable of serving as a counterweight to the Islamists—to negotiate an acceptable transition arrangement with the opposition coalition. The army has historically played a vital role as a bulwark against Islamism.

Washington should also give ElBaradei as wide a berth as possible. As Director General of the International Atomic Energy Agency, he revealed himself to be a prickly apologist for Iran's suspect nuclear activities who went out of his way to criticize the United States while obsequiously seeking to mollify Iran. Washington should instead seek to work with and bolster other secular opposition parties and emerging leaders of civil society. The immediate goal should be to assist the army in brokering a political deal that will enable a smooth transition to a sustainable democratic government that will not be subverted by the Muslim Brotherhood.

To this end, Washington should leverage its $1.5 billion in annual aid to Cairo to ensure the emergence of a government that respects the freedom and human rights of its own citizens and complies with Egypt's international obligations to fight terrorism, reject nuclear proliferation, and respect the peace treaty with Israel.

## The United States Should Continue to Support Freedom

Egypt's Muslim Brotherhood pursues a radical long-term Islamist agenda while masking its hostility to freedom and genuine democracy with self-serving tactical rhetorical moderation. The Obama Administration should patiently seek to advance freedom and stability in Egypt through a transition to a more representative government that gives the Muslim Brotherhood the smallest possible opportunity to hijack the reform process.

The worst possible outcome of the present crisis would be to open the door to a takeover by a totalitarian Islamist group hostile to the United States while working to replace President Mubarak's authoritarian regime.

> *"Throughout this period [of transition after President Mubarak's resignation], we should expect the Brotherhood to do what it has so often done: to work with, not against, the people whom it represents."*

# The Muslim Brotherhood Is Not a Threat to Democratic Change in Egypt

*David M. Faris and Stacey Philbrick Yadav*

*In the viewpoint that follows, David M. Faris and Stacey Philbrick Yadav argue that the Muslim Brotherhood has been a voice of progressive change in Egypt, one that led to the downfall of President Hosni Mubarak's repressive regime. Although the authors acknowledge that the Brotherhood has conservative ideals that stress the importance of Islam in national affairs, they contend the organization has never aimed to divide the country along sectarian lines but rather has been working mainly through charitable organizations to help all Egyptians during the decades of misrule. Faris and Yadav also point out that the Brotherhood is only one of many political factions in Egypt and has publically pledged that it will not seek to win the presidency in Egypt's new government.*

David M. Faris and Stacey Philbrick Yadav, "Why Egypt's Muslim Brotherhood Isn't the Islamic Bogeyman," *Christian Science Monitor*, February 14, 2011. Used by permission of the authors.

*Faris and Yadav urge the United States to relinquish its condemnation of the Brotherhood and work with all parties to bring democracy to Egypt. David M. Faris is a professor of political science at Roosevelt University in Illinois. Stacey Philbrick Yadav is a professor of political science at Hobart and William Smith Colleges in New York.*

As you read, consider the following questions:

1. According to Faris and Yadav, why has the Muslim Brotherhood been unfairly stigmatized as a violent organization?
2. What positive role has the Brotherhood played in the Egyptian parliament, as the authors relate?
3. As Faris and Yadav explain, how did Hosni Mubarak demonize the Muslim Brotherhood in order to win US support for his regime?

Before Egyptians had the chance to properly celebrate their tremendous victory and wake up to the first morning of a new Egypt [after President Hosni Mubarak stepped down on February 11, 2011], they were met with predictable concerns that Egypt is on the brink of an Islamist takeover. Western (particularly American) policymakers and pundits remain worried that Egypt's largest Islamist organization, the Muslim Brotherhood, will hijack the inspirational revolution that brought an end to Hosni Mubarak's 30-year tyranny, and will lead Egypt down the path of Iran-style theocracy.

By now, careful observers will know that these fears are unfounded on multiple levels. The protests were not led by the Muslim Brotherhood, which only joined them after they had been going on for days. The Brotherhood itself is not the bloodthirsty threat to liberty its enemies would have us believe. And the process of engaging in collective action may actually have deepened some of the internal fissures within the party's leadership, making it unlikely to "dominate" Egypt's future in any single, clear direction.

The Brotherhood is an organization whose leadership's main aim is to retain the ability to influence the shape of Egyptian society. This means that it will need to work with the military, along with Egyptians of all political backgrounds, to navigate a period of martial law before anticipated reforms take effect. Throughout this period, we should expect the Brotherhood to do what it has so often done: to work with, not against, the people whom it represents.

## The Brotherhood Is Like Any Other Political Organization

Over the past few weeks, those people have unequivocally told the Brotherhood, as they have told Mr. Mubarak, the Americans, and anyone who will listen, that they are finished with authoritarianism. On the barricades, they also rejected the logic of sectarianism. Brotherhood activists were among the many Muslims who protected Christians—and were protected by them—during the prayers in Tahrir Square and elsewhere that so eloquently and persistently spoke for freedom.

Some members of the Brotherhood participated in negotiations with Vice President [Omar] Suleiman, and pledged their support for Mohamed ElBaradei as a part of the National Association for Change, while others remained in the streets and in Tahrir, demanding no negotiation before Mubarak was gone. In other words, it is an organization that is responsive to its constituents' demands, but tactically divided in its pursuit of them.

So why do American policymakers and media analysts continue to be governed by a politics of fear? As the bogeyman of Egyptian politics, the Muslim Brotherhood has been labeled a terrorist organization, murderer of [former Egyptian President] Anwar Sadat, ally of [the terrorist organization] Al Qaeda, and the social equivalent of the Taliban [the Islamic organization that once controlled Afghanistan].

The reality is that the Brotherhood renounced violence decades ago, but the party's leadership and rank-and-file alike have continued to pay the cost of this now mistaken association, so carefully perpetuated by the Mubarak regime. Mr. Sadat's assassin came from a splinter organization called Egyptian Islamic Jihad (the group led by Ayman al-Zawahiri, who would later join forces with [al Qaeda leader] Osama Bin Laden). Most of Egypt's most unreconstructed militants, from Mr. Zawahiri's Islamic Jihad and the larger Islamic Group, remain in prison.

These are not the Brothers. In fact, the tiny cadre of real jihadists in Egypt scorns the Brotherhood as the "court Islamists" of the Mubarak regime, given that Brotherhood members have been repeatedly elected as independents to Egypt's parliament during Mubarak's rule. While this may play to committed militants as capitulation to a bankrupt regime, to most Egyptians, the Brotherhood's participation in parliament—particularly its dogged insistence on questioning ministers and holding the government to account—has helped to make an otherwise ornamental institution at least somewhat relevant.

Undoubtedly, this is why the Mubarak regime worked so hard to make sure that the Brotherhood's share of seats dropped from 88 to one in last November's election. When anticipated changes take effect and the Brotherhood is allowed to stand as a political party, it will join a wide range of other Islamist parties in the region (like Morocco's Justice and Development Party, Jordan's Islamic Action Front, and Yemen's Islah Party), whose participation has helped to make often anemic legislatures more significant, against all odds.

## The Brotherhood Is Diverse and Divided

Beyond this explicitly political role, however, the Brotherhood is probably better known and respected for its charitable work, which includes running hospitals, fund-raising, and other activities that are vital to many in Egypt, where millions live on less than two dollars a day. As the Mubarak regime's economic reforms increased the wealth of a small middle class, most Egyptians have seen their declining living standard accompanied by a shrinking social safety net, making the Brotherhood's welfare policies all the more critical in the lives of citizens in the Middle East's most populous country. The physical and economic damage wrought by the 18-day revolution will probably make this need even more plain.

When we lived in Cairo, we met and interviewed many Brothers (and Sisters) who were young, tech-savvy democrats— socially conservative for sure, but nothing like the cartoonish fanatics they are said to be in the West. They believe in Islam, but they also work in concert with Christians, leftists, and activists from other movements.

But some Brotherhood members have mixed feelings about the youth's confrontations with the regime, as reflected by the 2010 internal election of the relatively staid Mohammed Badie. This cadre appears to have expressed its reluctance mainly by re-investing its energies in the service activity that helped to build the organization in the first place, making sure that the social message doesn't get lost in the noise of opposition politics.

The Brotherhood probably commands the loyalty of more Egyptians than any other organized social or political force. But it is far from the only source of organized political opposition. Just how many parliamentary seats the Brotherhood would command in free and fair elections is unknowable, since Mubarak's regime has spent decades making sure that there are no organized political forces that might challenge state power.

But the organization has pledged publicly not to run a candidate in the coming presidential election, and it is not clear that they would pursue or be able to win a clear parliamentary majority. And yet the specter of an Islamist "takeover" has for too long been deployed against on-the-ground realities to justify continuing suppression of the democratic aspirations of all Egyptians— Muslim and Christian, Islamist, leftist, or liberal.

## The United States Should Support Peaceful Change

Any post-Mubarak Egyptian future that is not built on coercion is going to include the Muslim Brotherhood. Mubarak's regime long used fear of this alternative as a two-pronged strategy to divide the opposition, and convince the West that Mubarak and his allies were the only things standing between Egypt and an Iranian-style form of tyranny. Deliberately lumping all Islamist groups together in the popular imagination ensured that, in times of uncertainty, Washington sided with the status quo.

The [Barack] Obama administration's refusal to openly side with the protesters early in the crisis proved that fears of the Brotherhood still trump America's ostensible commitment to liberty. While the regime's decision to unleash violence on the protesters convinced Obama's splintered foreign policy team to work toward Mubarak's departure, more is needed to undo the damage of the administration's early wavering.

Under Mubarak, Egypt's authoritarian state has included an estimated 1.3 million internal security agents, collectively responsible for a level of brutality that is a far greater threat to Egyptian liberty than any paranoid fantasy about a Brotherhood takeover. With the US sending well over $1 billion in military aid to Cairo every year, the boots on the throats of Egypt's citizens for so long belonged as much to us as they did to Mubarak. This oppression, not the dollars, was the real cost of supporting the Egyptian regime.

The United States now has the opportunity to form a relationship with a new Egypt, built on mutual dignity and respect. Even with Mubarak's reign over, Egyptians deserve a clearer message of support from the US as they work to sweep away the remnants of his regime. The US must make a clean break with its politics of fear by supporting the Brotherhood's participation in the swift and genuine transition to democratic rule promised by the Egyptian Armed Forces. The Egyptian people ask for nothing more, and our ideals demand nothing less.

*"Alarmists would have us believe
that we are on the brink of another
Iran-style Islamist takeover, with the
destruction of Israel as its obsession.
The complacent, meanwhile,
dangerously understate the threat."*

# The Muslim Brotherhood's Role in Democratic Change in Egypt Remains Unclear

*Maajid Nawaz*

*In the following viewpoint, Maadjid Nawaz, a former political prisoner in Egypt and the current director of Quilliam, an anti-extremism think tank, argues that the Muslim Brotherhood is neither the terrifying bogeyman of Western fears nor the docile progressive party it seems to portray. To Nawaz, the truth lies somewhere in between: the Muslim Brotherhood does not have the popular backing to seize power if Egypt is left to determine its own fate, yet its conservative Islamic ideals are still radical enough to destabilize Egypt if the Brotherhood surged in popularity in response to Western intrusiveness. In Nawaz's opinion, the West should be wary of the Brotherhood but rely on the pro-reform mindset of Egyptians*

Maajid Nawaz, "The Post-Islamist Future," *Wall Street Journal*, vol. 257, no. 40, February 18, 2011. All rights reserved. Reproduced by permission.

*and the anti-Islamist suspicions of their military to counterbalance the threat and perhaps steer the country toward democracy.*

As you read, consider the following questions:

1. What is the Muslim Brotherhood's rallying cry, as Nawaz states?
2. According to Nawaz, why did many of the disaffected youth desert the Muslim Brotherhood in recent years?
3. According to a poll by the Washington Institute for Near East Policy, cited by the author, what percent of the popular vote did Muslim Brotherhood candidates receive in their bid for the presidency of Egypt?

Recent events in Egypt indicate the beginning of the end for the Middle East's fascination with Islamist opposition politics. Egypt's revolution is no deathblow to Islamism—it is not even a debilitating injury. But when thinking in terms of decades-long trends, it is the start of a new intellectual era for the region.

The 1950s and '60s witnessed the rise of pan-Arab socialism. Autocratic strongmen brought in by military coups were the order of the day in Egypt, Syria and beyond. By the 1980s and '90s, there was a fierce explosion in angry Islamism, as seen in the jihadist insurrection in Egypt and the rise of both Hamas [of Palestine] and Hezbollah [of Lebanon].

But with failed Islamist experiments in Iran, Sudan and Afghanistan, the new millennium saw a creeping transition. As I did, the region's young, tech-savvy youth developed new ambitions, away from Islamism and toward secular democratic politics. Democratic activism is the new political fashion.

## Western Fears of the Muslim Brotherhood

Naturally, the potential for democracy in Egypt has raised fears that Islamists will take over, establishing a popular yet anti-

Western and anti-Israel leadership. Being the most organized opposition group, the Muslim Brotherhood is the focus of these fears.

Alarmists would have us believe that we are on the brink of another Iran-style Islamist takeover, with the destruction of Israel as its obsession. The complacent, meanwhile, dangerously understate the threat. Interestingly, they are the very same voices who argued as recently as a month ago [January 2011] that the Brotherhood represents the only credible opposition in Egypt. Somewhere in the middle stand reasonable voices calling for critical engagement.

The Brotherhood is still formally committed to some of the more worrying Islamist principles of Hassan al-Banna, who founded the organization in 1928. Its popular rallying cry is "Allah is our objective; the Prophet is our leader; the Quran is our constitution; Jihad is our way; and death for the sake of Allah is the highest of our aspirations." And it insists that Islam must be the only source of legislation, and that non-Muslims and women cannot become heads of state.

The group's official line, therefore, inspires little confidence, especially as its current leader is the conservative Muhammad Badie (who was a cellmate of mine in 2002, when I was held as a political prisoner in Cairo's Mazra Tora prison). However, with a reformist middle-aged faction—led by another former cellmate of mine, Abdul Monim Aboul Fatouh—and a disillusioned youth, the Brotherhood is certainly no monolith.

## Younger Members Desert the Brotherhood

United by the popular imperative to remove [Egyptian President] Hosni Mubarak, the group rarely allowed dissent. Despite this, in 1996 a group of prominent but frustrated younger members broke off, founding *Hizb al-Wasat* (the Center Party), which included among its founders Christians, unveiled women and non-Islamists. The Brotherhood's old guard reacted dismissively, but it seems that the founders of the Center Party were years ahead of the curve.

Last year [in 2010], the Brotherhood had heated internal elections and middle-aged reformists were expected to do well. But under shady circumstances, and to the dismay of many frustrated younger members, they lost their seats at the leadership council. Things have never quite been the same.

Many younger Brotherhood activists, including friends of mine who had been jailed and tortured for their affiliation, froze their membership and joined the ranks of Egypt's increasingly bold secular youth activists. The groups included the Egyptian Movement for Change and the April 6th Youth. The effect was that the Brotherhood had to play catch-up when these secular democratic forces led the way in the January 25 uprising. The simple fact is that Egypt's most organized opposition group did not organize Egypt's only people's revolt. In addition, it is clear that the Brotherhood has no [Iranian leader Ayatollah] Khomeini-like figure capable of hijacking this revolution.

A recent poll by the Washington Institute for Near East Policy found that Muslim Brotherhood leaders received barely 1% of Egyptians' support for the presidency. Only 7% of respondents believed that "the [Mubarak] regime is not Islamic enough." This suggests that the Brotherhood is likely to win some seats in parliament but unlikely to produce the next president or prime minister of Egypt.

## A Moderate, Wait-and-See Approach

How, then, should policy makers think of the Brotherhood?

In a recent hearing of the U.S. House Intelligence Committee, Director of National Intelligence James Clapper asserted that the Brotherhood is a "largely secular" group. Such blunders are grossly counterproductive, as they hinder the clarity of understanding needed to plan for various contingencies, like Islamist ascendancy.

On the other hand, the alarmist approach—taken by many in Israel, for example—would seem to trade long-term regional security for short-term stability. As the former George W. Bush administration official Elliott Abrams remarked, "the Israelis apparently do not see the irony that they are mourning the departure of the man [Mubarak] who created the very situation they now fear." (Returning to the recent Washington Institute poll, more Egyptians supported peace with Israel than rejected it, and only 18% approved of either Hamas or Iran.)

British Prime Minister David Cameron and former Prime Minister Tony Blair have taken a more cautious and reasonable approach. In his groundbreaking speech in Munich, Mr. Cameron declared, "I simply don't accept that there's a dead-end choice between a security state and Islamist resistance." And concerning the risk of a Brotherhood takeover, Mr. Blair said that "The truth is I don't know and neither does anybody else. And therefore what I am really saying is, don't be hysterical about it but don't be complacent about it either."

As long as we engage all peaceful opposition forces with our eyes open, Egypt can become a beacon for Arab democracy. Like Turkey's, Egypt's largely secular army is wary of an Islamist takeover. If we can help Egyptians build a democratic society for the first time in their history, we may see the dawn of a new post-Islamist age that transforms political dynamics world-wide.

> *"[Arab Knesset member Ahmad] Tibi*
> *knows that no Arab country would*
> *afford him the freedoms that the Jewish*
> *state does."*

# Israel Is the Only True Democracy in the Middle East

*Jacob Dayan*

*Jacob Dayan serves as consul general of Israel in Los Angeles. In the viewpoint that follows, Dayan refutes the accusations of Ahmad Tibi, an Arab member of the Israeli parliament who has disparaged Israel as racist and fascist. Dayan points out that only in Israel, a true democracy, can Tibi's oppositional rhetoric be voiced without fear of government reprisal. Because Israel is a democracy, Dayan argues, all people—whether Muslim, Christian, or Jew—can voice their opinions freely. Dayan also states that all citizens can enjoy the benefits of education, unrestricted travel, and access to all public services precisely because Israel protects the rights of the population without discrimination based on creed or religion. Dayan claims that such democratic liberties are not available in many Arab nations, making Israel the only democracy in the Middle East.*

Jacob Dayan, "Yes, Israel's a Democracy," *Los Angeles Times*, May 27, 2010. Used by permission of the author.

As you read, consider the following questions:

1. Who have denied Palestinians their rights and citizenship, according to Dayan?

2. As Dayan states, by what percentage has the literacy rate of Israeli Arabs jumped between 1961 and 2010?

3. Why does the author believe it is a significant testament to Israel's democracy that Israeli Arabs can travel to Gaza?

The Jewish state of Israel is a diverse nation that has absorbed people from more than 140 countries. Among its population are about 1.5 million Arabs, including Israeli Knesset [parliament] member Ahmad Tibi, who in a May 23 [2010, *Los Angeles*] *Times* interview lashed out at Israel, using inflammatory words like "racist" and "fascist." As is his style, Tibi failed to back up his white-hot rhetoric with hard facts.

## Opportunities for All in Israel

In 1947, Arab leaders rejected a United Nations resolution to form an Arab state alongside a Jewish one. This caused the displacement of some 600,000 Palestinian refugees. From that point forward, Arab nations have denied these Palestinians and their descendants citizenship and basic civil rights, including the right to own property, get an education or take out loans—rights held by Israeli Arabs.

Arab Israelis, who make up about 20% of the nation's population, enjoy equal rights, government representation and protection in Israel. They live freely in all parts of Israel, can use all public facilities, attend Israel's top universities and are contributing members of society. By no means is Israel the epitome of perfection, but we do aspire for equality for all our citizens. According to the Abraham Fund Initiative, since Israel's establishment in 1948, the number of schools in the Arab Israeli school system increased by more than fifteenfold; Hebrew schools grew by only five times. The number of classes offered in

## No Racial or Religious Separation in Israel

Jewish and Arab babies are born in the same delivery room, with the same facilities, attended by the same doctors and nurses, with the mothers recovering in adjoining beds in a ward. Two years ago I had major surgery in a Jerusalem hospital: the surgeon was Jewish, the anaesthetist was Arab, the doctors and nurses who looked after me were Jews and Arabs. Jews and Arabs share meals in restaurants and travel on the same trains, buses and taxis, and visit each other's homes.

*Benjamin Pogrund, "Israel Is a Democracy in Which Arabs Vote," Focus, December 2005.*

the Arab Israeli system increased more than seventeenfold, and since 1961 the literacy rate of Arab Israelis jumped from 49.6% to 90%, a clear indication of the educational opportunities offered to all our citizens.

Not only are Arabs treated equally as individual citizens, but their minority status is also recognized in some aspects by the government, with Arabic being an official language in Israel (alongside Hebrew) and Israeli Muslims having their own jurisdiction on religious issues (Sharia law) pertaining to members of their community, just like Jewish religious law at the Rabbinical courts. Additionally, Arab Israelis are citizens with full voting rights and can serve as elected members of the Knesset, as lawmaker Tibi does. It is true that Arab Israelis hold about 10% of the Knesset seats, a number that is disproportionate to their population. Perhaps this is because Arab Israelis are opting instead to vote for non-Arab parties or exercising their democratic right not to vote at all.

## Freedom of Dissent and Expression

In his interview, Tibi made it clear that he has no intention of serving as a bridge between Israeli Arabs, Palestinians and Israeli Jews. But he also made it clear that he would never give up his Israeli citizenship or passport for a future Palestinian identity. And why would he? Would a Palestinian parliament allow a member to travel freely to an enemy state, such as the Arab Knesset members' recent public visit to Libya? Would a Palestinian parliament allow one of its members to serve as an adviser to a hostile government? For those who may not know, Tibi served as [deceased Palestine Liberation Organization leader] Yasser Arafat's adviser on Israeli affairs while simultaneously serving as a member of the Knesset.

Tibi knows that no Arab country would afford him the freedoms that the Jewish state does. After all, Arab Knesset members are even allowed to travel to Gaza [a Palestinian territory on the southern border of Israel], which is controlled by Hamas, the terrorist organization that vows to exterminate the Jewish state. Israeli Arab lawmakers travel there to express their support, then return to their Knesset offices to make their case to Israeli and international media. Is any such freedom available in the Arab world? Of course not! Tibi knows this; he relies on such freedoms to do his work.

Finally, allow me to reference Ishmael Khaldi who was—until recently—Israel's deputy consul general in San Francisco. Khaldi is a Bedouin who now serves as an adviser to Israeli Foreign Minister Avigdor Lieberman; he will visit Los Angeles in June [2010] to speak about his personal experiences. Below is an excerpt from what he said in a *San Francisco Chronicle* interview in March 2009:

> I am a proud Israeli—along with many other non-Jewish Israelis such as Druze, Baha'i, Bedouin, Christians and Muslims, who live in one of the most culturally diversified societies and the only true democracy in the Middle East. . . . By

any yardstick you choose—educational opportunity, economic development, women and gay's rights, freedom of speech and assembly, legislative representation—Israel's minorities fare far better than any other country in the Middle East.

I may not agree with Tibi's comments, but I do recognize the importance of his right to express his opinions. The freedom of expression, granted to Tibi by the only democratic state in the Middle East, is one that is also enjoyed by all Israeli citizens—Jews and Arabs alike.

| "Israel's apartheid policies toward Palestinians hardly qualify it as a democracy, much less the only one in the Middle East."

# Israel Is Not an Example of Democracy in the Middle East

*Josh Ruebner*

*In the following viewpoint, Josh Ruebner argues that Israel is a democracy in name only. According to Ruebner, Israel's repression of Palestinian Arabs—both in Israel and in the occupied territories—reveals that Israel has created a divided society in which Jews are privileged with full citizenship while Arabs often have their loyalty questioned, their organizations investigated, and their efforts to achieve self-rule undone. In Ruebner's opinion, the wave of democratic protests in Arab countries suggests that many Arab lands may become more liberal than Israel, leaving the Jewish state an obsolete relic of an age that tolerated ethnocracies. Josh Ruebner is the national advocacy director of the US Campaign to End the Israeli Occupation, a collective of organizations working to change US policy toward Israel to ensure respect for international law and human rights.*

Josh Ruebner, "The 'Only Democracy in the Middle East?' Hardly," *Huffington Post*, March 9, 2011. Used by permission of the author.

As you read, consider the following questions:

1. As Ruebner states, how did the war on terror provide Israel with a new legitimacy in the eyes of US policy makers?
2. What right has Israel denied to Palestinian refugees, according to Ruebner?
3. What two nations does Ruebner invoke to counteract Israel's claim that it is the only democracy in the Middle East?

Ever since Israel began to transition from a charity case to a strategic partner of the United States—an evolutionary process from the mid-1950s to the early 1970s—its supporters in the U.S. political arena have brandished a variety of arguments to justify the unusually close relationship.

From Egyptian President Gamal Abdul Nasser's Czech arms deal and subsequent embrace of the Soviet Union in 1955 until the dissolution of the bipolar superpower system in 1991, Israel's supporters maintained that this Western bastion served U.S. interests by thwarting the advance of Communism in the Middle East.

The abrupt end of the Cold War necessitated a new argument, and the rising lethality of transnational terrorism in the 1990s and 2000s provided one: Israel and the United States shared a common enemy and struggle in the "war on terror." In a shell-shocked post-9/11 political environment, this talisman did the trick well for a time. Israeli Prime Minister Ariel Sharon encapsulated this meme just two days after September 11, declaring to Secretary of State Colin Powell that Palestinian Authority President Yasser Arafat "is our Bin Laden."

## Israel Is an Obstacle to US Influence in the Middle East

However, as post-9/11 U.S. wars against and occupations of Iraq and Afghanistan wore on inconclusively, this argument lost a

## A Democracy for the Masters

Israel is definitely not a democracy. A country that occupies another people for more than 40 years and disallows them the most elementary civic and human rights cannot be a democracy. A country that pursues a discriminatory policy against a fifth of its Palestinian citizens inside the [19]67 borders cannot be a democracy. In fact Israel is what we use to call in political science a herrenvolk democracy, it's democracy only for the masters. The fact that you allow people to participate in the formal side of democracy, namely to vote or to be elected, is useless and meaningless if you don't give them any share in the common good or in the common resources of the State, or if you discriminate against them despite the fact that you allow them to participate in the elections.

*Ilan Pappé, interviewed by Frank Barat,*
*"An Interview with Ilan Pappé: Why Israel*
*Is Not a Democracy,"* Uruknet.info, *April 2,*
*2011. www.uruknet.info.*

great deal of its initial salience. With Israel unable to play more than a behind-the-scenes technological and intelligence role in supporting U.S. war efforts, and with the Muslim world rejecting Israel's ongoing colonization of Palestinian land and its brutal treatment of Palestinians living under its illegal military occupation, U.S. military leaders began to note that Israel actually is a drag on the "war on terror."

In his previous position as Commander of U.S. Central Command [CENTCOM], General David Petraeus testified to the Senate Armed Services Committee last year [2010] that "Arab anger over the Palestinian question limits the strength and depth of U.S. partnerships with governments and peoples in the AOR [Area of Responsibility of CENTCOM] and weakens the legitimacy of moderate regimes in the Arab world. Meanwhile, al-Qaeda and other militant groups exploit that anger to mobilize support."

Petraeus's testimony deflated the argument that Israel is a strategic asset to the United States, prompting Israel's supporters to rely increasingly on its remaining rationale that as the "only democracy in the Middle East," the United States and Israel share a common value system.

## Full Rights for the Privileged

This claim has always been disingenuous, ahistorical, and tinged with racism. Israel can claim to be a democracy only in the sense that apartheid South Africa could also claim to be so: an "ethnocracy" with full democratic rights for the privileged race or religion; lesser or no democratic rights for those with undesirable skin color, ethnicity, nationality, or race.

Israel became a preponderantly Jewish state, thereby gaining this veneer of democracy, only by ethnically cleansing indigenous Palestinians from their homes in 1948 and preventing to this day these refugees and their descendants from exercising their right of return to their homes as guaranteed by the Universal Declaration of Human Rights.

Palestinians who remained on their land and became citizens of Israel lived under martial law until 1966 and did not achieve even nominal equal rights until then. While enjoying the right to vote and run for office, Palestinian citizens of Israel—who comprise about 20 percent of the population—continue to face a bevy of official discriminatory laws and widespread societal racism that makes them second-class citizens analogous to African Americans in the Jim Crow South.

Since 1967, Israel has militarily occupied the Palestinian West Bank, East Jerusalem, and the Gaza Strip, placing four million Palestinians under harsh rule, suppressing their right to self-determination and foreclosing on their ability to live under their own free and democratic governance.

Today, even the limited rights afforded by Israel's "ethnocracy" are under threat. Its Jewish and Palestinian citizens find their rights circumscribed by proposed loyalty oaths, parliamentary investigations of nongovernmental organizations critical of the governmental line, and imprisonment of activists standing in solidarity with nonviolent Palestinian protestors in the occupied West Bank.

## Other Democracies in the Region

Israel's apartheid policies toward Palestinians hardly qualify it as a democracy, much less the only one in the Middle East. Since the Taif Agreement effectively ended Lebanon's civil war in 1989, the fragile country has had a functioning, although uniquely sectarian, parliamentary democracy. The withdrawal of Syrian troops from Lebanon in 2005, whose presence Israel's supporters used to discredit the independence of Lebanon's democratic system, made it difficult, if not impossible, to argue that Lebanon is not a democracy.

In addition, Israel's one-time strongest ally in the region—Turkey—has a long-standing democratic history. Although punctuated intermittently by military coups, Turkey has been coup-free since the military's "soft coup" of 1997 forced out Welfare Party Prime Minister Necmettin Erbakan.

And, after living through decades of tyranny, sanctions, wars, and occupation, Iraq appears to be emerging from the wreckage with a functioning multi-party parliamentary democracy, although facing severe challenges to its consolidation. This accomplishment is occurring despite, not because of, the bait-and-switch rationale for the U.S. war on Iraq that made democracy promotion a hasty afterthought once the ballyhooed weapons of mass destruction proved phantasmagorical.

Thus, even before pro-democracy and freedom movements began to inundate the Arab world in January 2011, Israel's claim to be "the only democracy in the Middle East" was tendentious, if not altogether spurious. However, the grassroots movements that have swept away dictators in Tunisia and Egypt, are on the verge of upending republican and monarchical tyrannies in Libya, Yemen, and Bahrain, and are making strong showings in Morocco, Algeria, and Jordan and have completely pulled the rug out from under the racist claims of Israel's supporters.

Never far from the surface of Israel's claim to be the "only democracy in the Middle East" was the implication that Arabs were unamenable to or incapable of practicing democracy. The willingness of hundreds of thousands of Arab protestors in the streets of Tunis, Cairo, Tripoli, Manama, and beyond to brave (often U.S.-equipped) armed forces to demand democracy—and for hundreds, if not thousands, to pay the ultimate price for doing so—has demolished this bigoted argument for good. While transitions to democratic governments are far from assured at this point, no one can claim again that Arabs do not yearn for democracy.

## Israeli Repression Cannot Last for Long

To even the most casual observer unaware of Israel's apartheid policies toward Palestinians, Israel's pretensions to democracy suddenly do not look very unique in the region. True, as long as the United States maintains its unconditional diplomatic and military support for Israel's policies, the international community will find it difficult, if not impossible, to sanction Israel for its violations of human rights norms a la apartheid-era South Africa. The [Barack] Obama Administration's first-ever veto in the Security Council last month of a draft resolution condemning Israel's illegal settlements illustrates this dynamic of the United States shielding Israel from unanimous international opposition to its policies.

However, as autocratic regimes in the Middle East are overthrown and democracies hopefully are firmly implanted, the days of Israel's ability to impose its apartheid rule on Palestinians are inevitably numbered. Truly democratic Arab regimes will never agree—as did Hosni Mubarak's Egypt—to acquiesce to and benefit from U.S. policies that make them co-sponsors of Israel's repression of Palestinians. Israel and its supporters know this full well, which is why they are hoping against hope that the tide of democracy in the Arab world is stemmed.

If democracy sweeps aside tyranny throughout the region, then Israel will stand as an isolated apartheid relic of a bygone era—much like Ian Smith's Rhodesia in postcolonial Africa—that is doomed to obsolescence. If the United States wants to be a true friend of Israel, then it will do its utmost to ensure Israel's transition to a real democracy by insisting on a just and lasting peace that includes equality for all Palestinians, whether they are refugees, citizens of Israel, or under occupation.

# Periodical Bibliography

*The following articles have been selected to supplement the diverse views presented in this chapter.*

Allan C. Brownfeld

"In the Middle East's 'Only Democracy,' Some Jews Are More Equal than Others," *Washington Report on Middle East Affairs*, May-June 2010.

John J. Di Iulio Jr.

"Authentic Democracy," *America*, March 21, 2011.

Hillel Fradkin and Lewis Libby

"Egypt's Islamists: A Cautionary Tale," *Commentary*, April 2011.

Abdullah Gul

"The Revolution's Missing Peace," *New York Times*, April 21, 2011.

Abigail Hauslohner and Shahira Amin

"Democracy, Egyptian Style," *Time*, April 18, 2011.

Matthew Kaminski

"Among the Muslim Brothers," *Wall Street Journal*, April 9, 2011.

Fania Oz-Salzberger

"But Is It Good for Democracy?," *World Affairs*, May-June 2010.

Assem Safieddine and Leila Atwi

"Is Governance a Prerequisite for Democracy? Insights from the Middle East," *Middle East Policy*, Spring 2009.

Oliver Schlumberger

"Opening Old Bottles in Search of New Wine: On Nondemocratic Legitimacy in the Middle East," *Middle East Critique*, Fall 2010.

Richard Wolin

"A Fourth Wave Gathers Strength in the Middle East," *Chronicle of Higher Education*, February 18, 2011.

Fareed Zakaria

"The Revolution," *Time*, February 14, 2011.

OPPOSING
VIEWPOINTS®
SERIES

CHAPTER 3

# What Should Be Done to Improve US Democracy?

# Chapter Preface

In the following chapter, Eric Alterman, a fellow at the progressive public policy think tank, the Center for American Progress, claims that American democracy is plagued with problems including the undue influence of special interest groups and the lackluster participation of voters. Even the electoral process itself has been called into question. Most notably, when voters did turn out in the 2000 presidential race between Republican nominee George W. Bush and Democratic Vice President Al Gore, controversy arose around the method in which America elects its chief executive. In the United States, the president is chosen by members of the Electoral College, a body of representatives chosen by each state to formally endorse a candidate chosen by the voters in the state. In all but two US states, all the electoral votes (the number varies per state) are commonly awarded to the candidate who wins the popular vote in that state. For that reason, candidates tend to favor campaigning in "swing states"—those in which the outcome of the votes is not assured going into the race—to achieve the number of electoral votes needed to secure victory. They also focus on the states with the most electoral votes, such as California, Florida, and New York. Under the current system, candidates may squeak by with a small margin of popular votes in those states and win the presidency, even if they lost by a large margin in multiple states with fewer electoral votes. Thus it is possible that the aggregate popular vote of the nation could endorse one candidate while the votes of the Electoral College elect the opposing candidate. According to the results of the 2000 presidential race, Bush won 271 Electoral College votes and Gore received 266 (one electoral voter refused to cast a vote in the official tally). Bush lost the nationwide popular vote by .5 percent, yet because he won more electoral votes, he was awarded the victory. The uncertainty that prevailed following the election and the discrepancy between the popular vote and the awarding of Electoral College votes has prodded some critics, such as liberal talk show host Bill Press, to call for an end to the College. In a CNN editorial on November 8, 2000, Press argued, "it is an insult to democracy for a candidate to win the popular vote, yet lose the election and the presidency, because of the electoral college."

In addition to questions about the method of presidential election, much has been made about the dominance of the two-party system in the United States. Partisanship, a phenomenon in which politicians vote strictly along party lines and rarely work with individuals from the opposing party to develop legislation or make political decisions, has effectively handcuffed the government on some occasions. Congressional majorities of a specific party ensure that bills of the ruling party pass while the bills of the opposition party do not. In some instances, the majority in one house of Congress is different than the majority in the other, resulting in stalled legislation. Writing in a March 2010 online commentary, *American Prospect* cofounder and coeditor Robert Kuttner noted, "A number of smart commentators . . . have aptly observed that we now have a semi-parliamentary system, in which the opposition party can block but the governing party can't govern." Views such as this one have become prominent in the discussion about the state of American democracy and have led many to believe that the system is broken and must be reformed if it is to provide legitimate governance for all Americans.

Whether the system ignores the will of the people or ties up meaningful change in partisan politics, the country has not abandoned these mainstays of American democracy. Yet many observers, including Alterman, insist that this democracy is in decline. In the chapter that follows, commentators offer their views on the state of US democracy and offer suggestions of possible reforms that they believe might correct this trend.

> "We need a system that has fairer rules,
> that diminishes the role of money
> and that encourages politicians and
> journalists to investigate and portray
> the realities they observe honestly,
> thereby reducing the distorting lenses of
> finance, ideology and ignorance."

# American Democracy
# Is Broken

*Eric Alterman*

*In the viewpoint that follows, Eric Alterman contends that US democracy is in need of serious reform if it is to continue to function as a governing mechanism for and by the people. Alterman focuses on several main problems that have plagued the system in recent years including the poorly functioning Senate, the unwillingness of politicians to enact change, the immense influence of lobbyists and special interest groups, and voter participation and rights. Each of these issues, argues the author, contributes to the dysfunction of the US government and must be remedied to strengthen the nation's democracy. Eric Alterman is a fellow at the progressive public policy think-tank, the Center for American Progress, and author of the book* Kabuki Democracy: The System vs. Barack Obama.

Eric Alterman, "Kabuki Democracy—And How to Fix It," *Nation*, vol. 292, no. 4, January 24, 2011. All rights reserved. Reproduced by permission.

As you read, consider the following questions:

1. What does Alterman state to be the two main problems hindering the Senate from functioning properly?
2. What solution does the author suggest to alleviate the problem of institutional corruption?
3. How does the Australian practice of mandatory voting influence the politicians, as stated by Norman Ornstein and cited by the author?

It's no secret our democracy does not work well anymore. In many respects, including that particularly large swath of issues that involve someone's monetary profit and someone else's loss, it can barely be said to be a democracy at all—unless one takes the view held by some in Washington and Wall Street that money fulfills the function not only of free speech but of citizenship itself. If America is to ameliorate its current democratic dysfunction anytime soon, merely electing better candidates to Congress is not going to be enough. We need a system that has fairer rules, that diminishes the role of money and that encourages politicians and journalists to investigate and portray the realities they observe honestly, thereby reducing the distorting lenses of finance, ideology and ignorance. And yet these items rarely feature on any progressive agenda.

## US Democracy Needs Real Change

This is, in many ways, understandable. Ending the [George W.] Bush/[Dick] Cheney administration, and defeating the Christian conservative and corporate base on whose behalf it acted, required emergency measures of a largely defensive nature. And the chance to replace George W. Bush with Barack Hussein Obama both for symbolic and pragmatic reasons in 2008 appeared so enticing (and exciting) that we can all be forgiven for losing ourselves in the romance of focusing our time, money and energies on making this man America's forty-fourth president.

But the 2008 election was not a game changer after all. For change of the kind Obama promised and so many progressives imagined, we need to elect politicians willing to challenge the outdated rules of the Senate, fight for publicly financed elections and, in the absence of that, struggle against the Supreme Court's insistence on giving corporations the same free speech rights as individuals. We need smarter organizations that pressure politicians as well as pundits and reporters, not necessarily to see things our way but to hold true to the ideals they profess to represent. We must work to transform our culture to re-ennoble the notion of the "public good."

Some of the challenges standing in our way look to be all but impossible to overcome, like the blatant limitations on democracy inherent within the Electoral College or a Constitution that grants Wyoming and California the same power in the Senate. Others, meanwhile, are maddeningly complex, such as Senate rules regarding cloture and the like. But particularly in light of the 2010 election, apathy is no option. A little imagination and a great deal of hard work and patience can help put us on a path to a more democratic and equitable America. But don't expect it to be easy, and don't be surprised at the resistance of those who profit from politics as usual.

## The US Senate Functions Poorly

Congress has become a place where, most of the time, nothing much happens. Once in a great while, however, because of the political investments of one side or another, a massive piece of transformative legislation grows too big to fail and is somehow rammed through Congress without much concern for the parliamentary niceties that had up until that moment dominated the process. The Obama administration passed weakened versions of healthcare reform and financial regulation in this fashion but failed with cap and trade [an emissions trading policy aimed at limiting the amount of pollutants released into the atmosphere].

Most voters do not follow politics closely and hence remain largely uninformed about the precise nature of our system's dysfunction. This allows activists who work on specific issues to manipulate the process and shape legislation up to the final vote with hardly anyone paying attention. And although once upon a time partisans were satisfied to earn a legislator's nay vote, the new expectation has become to find a way to kill it.

Clearly, the secret hold that allows senators to delay business on any legislation for as long as they like deserves to die. The Senate has attempted to quash this practice. In a standoff that captures the absurdity of this body's method of self-policing, a 2006 bill to expose secret holds was itself the victim of a series of secret holds. To quote Oregon's Ron Wyden from the floor debate, "That pretty much says it all." Eventually, the Senate did pass the Honest Leadership and Open Government Act, which purported to end secret holds and demanded that senators stand by them in public. But, true to form, the act lacked any credible enforcement mechanism. It will likely change nothing. . . .

Bringing holds out into the open would subject them to public accountability and backlash. But the undemocratic ability of a single senator to stop most Senate business would remain. Apart from the unanimous consent procedure, party leaders generally choose to honor holds as evidence of a senator's threat to filibuster (even in cases where it seems obvious that a senator has little intention of making good on the threat). Countering that gridlock requires addressing the filibuster itself. Although rules surrounding filibusters are arcane, effective reform need not be. The key objective must be to preserve the legitimate tactic of reasonable delay by a dedicated minority to provide for more debate, more information and more public awareness about proposals that could soon carry the force of permanent law while preventing purposeful and permanent obstruction of majority rule. For example, the Patriot Act, which sailed through Congress in just four days during the panic after the September 11 attacks, would clearly have been a better law if a group of senators had been able to ensure that its most controversial aspects got a more thoughtful and thorough hearing. . . .

## Politicians Hinder Structural Reform

The reforms for these structural constraints, however, are hindered not only by the structural constraints themselves—like the Kafkaesque [senseless] secret hold on a bill to ban secret holds—but also by the character of the reform constituency. It's not easy to persuade incumbents to reform the system that they have worked so hard to game. As *Newsweek* columnist Ezra Klein notes, "They've got donor networks, relationships with lobbyists, corporate friends, and activist groups that will help them. Their challengers don't."

What's more, it can be awfully difficult to get media attention for process and precedent. And it's a rather significant challenge to convert the public disgust with Washington and concerns about corporate corruption of politics into informed support for procedural proposals that operate at least one layer apart from policies that affect people's lives. Finally, it is no simple matter to persuade good-government liberals to play the kind of hardball required to win the fights these reforms inevitably involve.

The severity of our political crisis may change some of these dynamics. For example, an unusual alliance of twenty-seven high-dollar donors went "on strike" for the first time in 2010, pledging to withhold donations from candidates unless they supported a public funding system for Congressional races. "I'd rather have campaign finance reform than access," explained one of the members, Steve Kirsch, a businessman who says he funneled more than $10 million to back Al Gore in 2000. The effort was organized by Change Congress, a group founded in 2008 by political consultant Joe Trippi and activist/legal scholar Lawrence Lessig. So far the numbers have been tiny compared with the flood of private spending that is swamping our system—which is understandable, as this is an awfully risky strategy to pursue when the other side refuses to play along. . . .

## Legalized Bribery Harms the Election Process

It is not so surprising that the problem of Senate reform comes down to the power of the purse, a problem the Supreme Court has greatly exacerbated in recent years with its corporate-friendly rulings in virtually all matters relating to money and speech. The most practical way to combat private financial influence in campaign funding is to reduce it. Yet as long as the Supreme Court continues to equate money with speech and corporations with people, legalized bribery will likely continue to corrupt the system. Absent an awakening on the part of a majority of Supreme Court justices, the only practical avenue to empowering the public interest in these battles is to subsidize campaigns. In this public funding system, candidates agree to cap their spending in exchange for government funding. The cost of campaigning drops, and the amount of money candidates accept from private donors is drastically reduced. And even though participation is voluntary, candidates are often eager to embrace it, given how much more enjoyable, to say nothing of convenient, it would be for them to cash a campaign check for a few million dollars than to endlessly work the phones begging rich folks for money.

Public funding is an elegant remedy to the problem of institutional corruption: instead of accepting legal bribes from donors in exchange for special consideration, candidates receive money from taxpayers in exchange for a pledge to spend less on their campaigns. And it works. Without much fanfare, public funding operated effectively for six consecutive elections, beginning in 1976, when candidates in both parties accepted funds and spending limits. The campaigns were cheaper, and the parties enjoyed relative financial parity. The parties split elections three to three during that period, and challengers beat incumbents in three out of the five races when incumbent presidents ran for re-election. . . .

But presidential elections are not the main problem. Congress is. And its members have proven quite adept at protecting their prerogatives, particularly when it comes to retaining their jobs. The House and Senate have taken a range of small steps to regulate campaigns in recent years. They agreed to ban companies and unions from directly contributing to candidates, capped the amount that individuals can give, limited the use of "soft money" by the parties and regulated how independent groups spend money on television commercials. Even though these restrictions have had some impact on the margins of a few elections, they are far from the main event. The truth is that even though Congress supports public funding for presidential campaigns, it continues to resist public funding for itself. This is understandable. On Capitol Hill incumbents enjoy a consistent fundraising advantage over their challengers, and they like it that way. As the late Senator Robert Byrd declared in 1987, "The need for Congressional campaign financing reform is obvious, but just because it is obvious does not mean that it is easy to attain.". . .

## The Conflict of Interests in Congress

A glaring conflict of interest for members of Congress and their staffs is the tempting prospect of quadrupling their salary with a job after government service if they keep these potential employers happy. President Obama kept his campaign pledge and formally banned most lobbyists from working in his administration. That rule acknowledged the revolving door between government and industry, but it stopped people only on the way into government and only within the executive branch. The rule did nothing to address Congress, where the real horse-trading takes place. After all, the problem is less whether lobbyists come to work in government, where pay is lower, hours longer and financial disclosure forms far more onerous, and more whether people leave government to cash in on their connections (and sometimes even to be paid off for services rendered). When the top staffer for the House Banking Committee jumps ship for Goldman Sachs in the middle of a big fight over the regulation of Goldman itself and can do so without violating any federal regulations, old-fashioned bribery becomes unnecessary.

Until 2007 federal law required government officials to wait just one year before taking jobs lobbying their former colleagues. When Congress extended the break to two years and applied the law to a wider circle of Congressional staff and administration officials, it drove one senator into early retirement. Trent Lott of Mississippi, a former Republican majority leader, quit, Sarah Palin–style, before his term was up just to ensure that he could cash in on his old job without bothering to wait an extra year. The new regulation was a start. Yet the goal cannot simply be to inconvenience the future Trent Lotts of the world. It must be to root out the encouragement the system offers to staffers to sell themselves to the highest bidder.

But again, how? We need a lobbying ban to insulate our elected officials and their top staffers from the temptation to sell themselves while doing the people's business and for a few years afterward. In business terms, ex-officials and their staffs need to be forced to protect their trade secrets and lay down robust non-compete clauses. A strong ban on employment with firms doing business under legislation covered by the elected officials and relevant staffers would need to run from eight to twelve years. . . .

## Anemic Voter Participation Rates Must Be Remedied

Another item on the long-term reform agenda needs to be the question of democracy itself. American politics, with its anemic participation rates, invites too much influence in our elections for too many undemocratic forces. As the American Enterprise Institute's Norman Ornstein has noted, to counter the oversized power of such minority interests, "in Australia, where failure to show up at the polls (you can vote for 'none of the above') leads to a $15 fine, attendance is over 95 percent—and politicians cater less to consultants and the extremes (since both bases turn out in equal proportions) and more to the small number of persuadable voters who are not swayed by outrageous rhetoric." A few right-wing libertarians might cry "totalitarianism," but most Americans would likely come to see mandatory voting as a reasonable way to ensure that everybody gets a say. After all, nobody's being forced to vote "for" anyone, just to affirm their bona fides as small-d democrats, which is an essential component of citizenship.

The short-term problem with mandatory voting, however, lies not in its demands on individuals but in the inability of municipalities to locate and register voters who are legally entitled to vote and identify those who are not. Australia, as it happens, puts most of the onus to register voters on election authorities. Australian election officials gather information from government agencies to identify unregistered eligible voters and mail them the requisite voting materials. In this respect Australia is not unusual; the United States is. For example, according to one survey of sixteen nations and four Canadian provinces, only four place the onus of voter registration entirely on the individual, as the United States does, which helps account for this country's anemic rates of political participation. The same goes for our unwillingness to allow people to vote on a weekend or a holiday, when they are not forced to miss work or to wait on line for hours merely to exercise their constitutional right to pick their leaders. (It is as if some politicians do not want people, particularly hourly wage workers, to be able to vote.) . . .

## Ex-Felons Should Be Allowed to Vote

A final item on this agenda for expanded and improved democracy needs to be the extension of the right to vote to ex-felons. Millions of Americans have had their right to vote revoked for periods ranging from the time spent incarcerated to a lifetime. In fourteen states a person can lose the right to vote for life. This is morally indefensible. In the United States the right to vote is not contingent on good behavior any more than it is on race, religion or ethnicity. And the idea that even after one has paid one's proverbial "debt to society," one must continue to pay with one's right to vote makes no moral or political sense. Most of these laws are rooted in the Jim Crow era and were intended to bar minorities from voting; many continue to operate that way, with black and Latino voters, particularly men, discouraged or prevented from voting in numbers well beyond their proportion in the population. What's more, as in the case of Florida in 2000, confusion regarding differing state felony disenfranchisement laws can easily result in eligible voters, sometimes even those with no disqualifying criminal conviction, being purged from the rolls or denied the ability to register to vote or cast their ballots. The provisions of the Democracy Restoration Act, introduced in Congress in July 2009 by Wisconsin Senator Russ Feingold and Michigan Representative John Conyers, would restore voting rights in federal elections to nearly 4 million Americans who have been released from prison and are living in the community, and would ensure that people on probation would not lose their right to vote. As a matter of fairness and strategy, this bill deserves the energetic support of all liberals and progressives.

Throughout our history, a more democratic America has consistently helped create a more progressive America, and these steps taken in support of improving democracy will likely help offset more reactionary developments in our political environment.

> *"Democracy is not about focusing on what the Congress is doing right now; it's about what we, the citizens who vote for the members of Congress, are doing."*

# American Democracy Is Not Broken

*T.A. Barnhart*

*Although many critics have decried the state of the US democracy, some citizens remain hopeful about the resiliency of the system and the people's active participation to maintain it. T.A. Barnhart expresses this sentiment in the following viewpoint as he argues that while the government may not be making all the decisions the people want at this moment, the strength of the US democracy lies in the people who take action by voting for new representatives who will enact the legislation their constituents support. Barnhart provides many examples of US citizens actively participating in the democratic process on local, state, and national levels. The author believes that as long as Americans continue to take an active role in the direction of the country, US democracy will remain strong and intact. T.A. Barnhart is a progressive blogger from Oregon and a regular contributor to the website BlueOregon.*

As you read, consider the following questions:

1.  What are some of the activities cited by the author that lead him to the conclusion that "Democracy is stronger than ever"?

2.  As stated by the author, what are the differences between the American democracy and the democracy of Zimbabwe?

3.  In what ways is democracy "a process, a journey, a state-of-mind and a state-of-being" as defined by the author?


A friend sent me a message on Facebook yesterday that included mourning for, as he put it, "our ebbing democracy." I understand his feelings, of course: with the [Iraq] invasion still on-going, telecom immunity, corporations running the world and a criminal [George W. Bush] sitting in the White House because of the SCOTUS [Supreme Court of the United States] Coup of 2000, mourning American democracy seems like a rational response.

Yet, as I replied to him, I believe our democracy has never been in better shape. We have much to celebrate this 4th of July [2008]. Despite the problems we face, I think the Founders would be both proud and excited by actions of American patriots as we move deeper into our country's third century. How can I make such a claim in the face of all the challenges we face? Easy: I'm paying attention not to the challenges but the responses.

## American Citizens Are Driving the Democratic Process

When all is going well, when people are fat and happy and life's circumstances aren't too bad for most people, complacency is an understandable human response. And until George W. Bush and his criminal gang came along, most Americans were complacent about our country's politics and the state of our democracy. People had jobs; not necessarily great jobs, but the bills got paid and there was a bit extra. Gas was cheap. The status quo was tolerable. Most people didn't get involved in politics because few people believed it mattered much what they did or said, so most people did or said little. I don't think most people would have said things were great, but things were acceptable enough for most Americans.

Then came the Bush coup, and then came 9/11, the invasion of Iraq and the attacks on Constitutional rights. Complacency was replaced by fear, and then fear itself became the new flavor of complacency. Where for so long a resigned acceptance of a tolerable state in society held fast, the new fear-based status quo began to have an effect. Some people became demoralized by the direction our nation was going. Others grew resigned to the inevitable— as that was defined by the White House. But millions of other Americans had a different response: They began to get angry.

With the Dean for America movement in 2003, American patriots who rejected both despair and apathy were encouraged to take back their country. Which they began doing, with growing success. The bitter losses of 2004 masked the growth of the progressive movement and the injection of millions of citizens into the political process. But 2004 became 2006, and more Americans got on-board with the idea that they were part of the democratic process—a victorious democratic (and Democratic) process. 2007 and 2008 saw Barack Obama pushed to the Democratic nomination and a record number of people voting in the primaries—every state's primary actually mattered, for the first time in history. Suddenly, in the midst of the darkness flooding out of Washington, DC and the corporate boardrooms the way darkness and horror emanated from Mordor and Isengard, something amazing has happened:

Democracy is stronger than ever.

What we've been seeing for the past five or six years is not a blip: it's a new way of thinking for millions of Americans. The message activist groups have been hammering for years—that every person, every vote, every donation matters—is not merely sinking in: It's bringing results. The candidates we-the-people support are winning elections, and then they are working to pass good legislation and oversee government on behalf of the 90% of Americans who are not wealthy and powerful. (Congress may not have gotten there yet, but other legislatures and governments, like the Oregon Leg of 2007, have made great progress for the majority of citizens.)

## Democracy Is Working

*Democracy is working*. Even with the ugliness we see in Congress, Wall Street and the federal courts, democracy is working. Look at Zimbabwe, where the voters were finally ready to get rid of a tyrant every bit as bad as [former leader of Iraq] Saddam [Hussein]: Instead, they got violence, bloodshed, the destruction of the main opposition party, and [Robert] Mugabe's re-election (such as it was). Here in America, with our democracy in allegedly so much trouble, we have a free and vigorous election that will—not might, but will—replace the illegitimate usurper with, quite likely, a skinny black guy whose parents could not have named him more awkwardly for national politics. Even the coup of 2000 was, I hate to admit, done legally and without violence—apart from that suffered by the body politic.

*Democracy is working*. Last Saturday [June 28, 2008], *too many* people showed up for the [Oregon youth voting organization] Bus Project's trip to Washington County: A bunch of young, active citizens—including Bus co-founder, Jefferson Smith—literally could not get on the Bus and instead had to take (bleah) cars out to Hillsboro to participate in the electoral process. Dozens of us, spending a beautiful Saturday not playing in the park but making sure democracy was moving forward.

*Democracy is working*. People are registering to vote for whom that act had before been seen as a waste of time. They are actually casting that vote, too, not just filling in the card and forget-

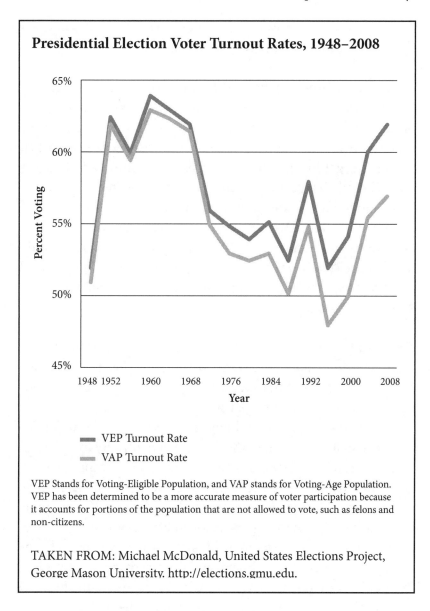

## Presidential Election Voter Turnout Rates, 1948–2008

━━ VEP Turnout Rate

▬▬ VAP Turnout Rate

VEP Stands for Voting-Eligible Population, and VAP stands for Voting-Age Population. VEP has been determined to be a more accurate measure of voter participation because it accounts for portions of the population that are not allowed to vote, such as felons and non-citizens.

TAKEN FROM: Michael McDonald, United States Elections Project, George Mason University. http://elections.gmu.edu.

ting about it. They are paying attention to the issues and voting for candidates who oppose the war, who are not going to kowtow to the corporations, who will work for universal health care. They are voting on the issues, and they are about to remake the

Congress and state governments in an overhaul that will over-shadow anything we have seen in our lifetimes.

*Democracy is working*. People aren't just voting: they are getting involved in the process. The Obama and [Hillary] Clinton campaigns (and Ron Paul's, for that matter) got the publicity for the numbers involved, but the phenomenon goes deep down-ticket. People are getting involved because it's dawning on them, as Dr. [Hillary] Dean said over and over, that they have the power. "Keep hope alive!" was Jesse Jackson's rallying cry in the '80s, and it seems to me that people *were* paying attention. They have hope for their country, and so they are getting to work to undo the damage that has been done. Progressives are taking control because progressives are doing the work where it matters most: down at the roots.

*Democracy is working*. It's alive, strong, growing and effective. It is also a process, a journey, a state-of-mind and a state-of-being. Democracy is not about focusing on what the Congress is doing right now; it's about what we, the citizens who vote for the members of Congress, are doing. Democracy is not about the laws that are in place (or, in the case of net neutrality or universal health care, not in place); it's about how we, the citizens, respond: either meekly accede to these laws or unite to challenge, remove and replace those laws. Democracy is not about the Supreme Court deciding that the rights of corporations outweigh those of actual human beings; democracy is about how we, the citizens for whom the 14th Amendment, and the rest of the Constitution, live our lives despite the attempts to make us the chattel of those who would profit from what goes on behind the Beltway.

## The Overwhelming Force of Democracy

Yes, we need to mourn what is being done by those to whom we, the American people, have given power and authority. But we, not they, are responsible for these failures. When the Gang of Five decided to throw away the results of the election in Florida, did we take to the streets and demand that every vote be counted? When Bush spread his transparent pack of lies to invade Iraq, how many citizens bothered to do more than let their fears overwhelm their sense (a bit late now, their remorse over the war)? How many of us turn off corporate television and the marketing/ brainwashing that transforms us into numb-witted sheep? How many keep their bodies healthy so their minds and spirits will follow suit? How many sit in church and wonder why God is so often in agreement with the mere human being standing at the front?

For American democracy to ebb and fail, the citizens of the United States would have to give up belief in it and turn away from their civic responsibilities. This is not happening, and as a result, I say democracy has never been stronger, has never been in such great condition. Democracy is not the laws on the books, not the occupants of offices, nor the fluffstorms being raised by the corporate media. Democracy is that overwhelming force, that unshakeable foundation into which the Founders put their faith; the one institution and process so vital, so insurmountable our founding document, the Constitution, begins with the words that measure how weak or strong our democracy is, and upon which my own faith in the current condition of democracy rests:

"We, the people. . ."

| "A fair, across-the-board tax code would promote economic growth and broaden the tax base."

# To Improve US Democracy, Low-Income Workers Should Share the Income Tax Burden

*Mary Kate Cary*

*In the United States, individuals whose annual income exceeds a certain amount must pay a percentage to the federal government in the form of income taxes; others whose income falls below a certain level do not pay any income taxes. In the viewpoint that follows, Mary Kate Cary argues that this system is not only unsustainable in the face of increasing government spending, but even worse, harms US democracy. Cary suggests that the current tax code places an unfair burden on the minority of Americans who make the most money and in the process creates a divide between classes, which fosters resentment. Further she contends that the citizens who do not pay taxes do not have the same level of involvement and concern with how the government spends taxpayer money, and thus they are not as likely to hold politicians accountable for their choices. Cary recommends an even tax code requiring all Americans to pay a portion of their income to the government in the form of taxes to help remedy these problems and strengthen US democracy. Mary Kate Cary is a speechwriter who wrote speeches for George H.W. Bush and a regular contributor to* U.S. News & World Report.

As you read, consider the following questions:

1. As stated by the author, what percent of US households do not pay any federal income taxes?
2. According to Cary, how much more will the "average middle-class family" pay in federal taxes over the next ten years?
3. Cary states that the "class warfare rhetoric coming out of the White House" causes what negative repercussions in society?

I come from a typical middle-class family, but when it came time for college, financial trouble hit. My parents called a family meeting and told my siblings and me that we'd be putting ourselves through college. We went to state universities and service academies, took out loans, and worked at part-time jobs between classes.

At various times in college, I was a dishwasher, a librarian, and a complaint desk manager. I even worked in the underwear section at a men's shop (just what you want your 20-year-old daughter doing). Because I was working hard and paying my own tuition, I didn't take notoriously easy courses, buy brand-new textbooks, or sleep through morning classes. Kids waste their parents' college money all the time, but a funny thing happens when they're paying their own way: They suddenly become fiscal hawks.

Maybe if more college kids personally paid at least a portion of their own tuition bills, they'd hold a financial stake in seeing that things turn out well.

## Tax Cuts Cripple California

In the late 1990s when the dot-com boom boosted California's economy, state lawmakers increased spending by about $10 billion, mostly to play catch-up on K–12 education and to expand health and social services. But they also foolishly cut taxes by about $10 billion. When the boom busted, revenues fell, but Sacramento neither rolled back the tax cuts nor repealed the spending increases. Desperate for revenues, Gov. Gray Davis, a Democrat, in 2003 tripled the vehicle license fee, which generated $4 billion a year by boosting fees by $130 on a typical car. Schwarzenegger, a Republican, swept into office that same year in part by promising to roll back the unpopular increase in the "car tax." He kept his pledge and plunged the state into an even deeper budget crisis.

The . . . most important budget problem [though] is the fiscal straitjacket created by Proposition 13, the original tax-revolt ballot proposition that voters approved in 1978, which capped property taxes and made it extremely difficult to raise revenues.

*Donald Cohen and Peter Dreier,*
*"California in Crisis," American Prospect,*
*vol. 21, no. 2, March 2010.*

## Awareness of Money Fosters Responsibility

So, no postgrad tour of Europe for me: I worked to pay back my student loans at $66 a month, which was a big chunk of my $13,000-a-year salary as a receptionist for a congressman. I also started paying taxes on that $13,000. After withholding, I earned $750 a month—a grand total of $9,000 a year in take-home pay. (Granted, these were 1985 dollars.) Believe me, when roughly a third of your measly income goes to taxes, you are painfully aware of where your dollars are going and how the government spends them. Over time, you become very aware of where the next tax bracket lies, and you start making decisions about whether it's worth it to take a second job, continue to rent a house, and, later, whether to stay home with the baby.

Today, a person at my post-college income level would be exempt from paying taxes. That's because over the years, more and more Americans have been removed from the tax rolls. Earlier this week [April 2009], more than 40 percent of households did not have to write a check for any federal income tax at all. According to the Congressional Budget Office, the top 20 percent of taxpayers—whose average household pretax income of $250,000 drops to $180,000 after taxes—are paying 69 percent of all federal income taxes and a whopping 86 percent of all individual income taxes.

That may sound like a lot of income if you live in Indiana or Iowa. But if you live in New York City, Los Angeles, or Washington, it's something completely different. In some parts of America, $200,000 of household income makes you Bill and Melinda Gates. In others, it makes you the high school principal and your spouse a government employee.

## Pitting Americans Against Each Other

Under President Obama, that tax burden is about to increase exponentially. Even after putting his proposed tax hikes aside, the average middle-class family will pay an additional $200,000 in federal taxes over the next 10 years simply as service on Obama's $6.5 trillion in deficit spending, according to Michael Boskin, the former chairman of the Council of Economic Advisers under President George H.W. Bush. "In other words, a middle-aged, two-career couple in New York or California could get a future tax bill as big as their mortgage," he writes, because of massive government spending.

That strikes me as dangerous economically. At some point, the camel's back will break. Relying on a smaller and smaller minority of taxpayers to fund the cost of a massively sprawling government for millions of Americans is simply untenable. The rational economic decisions of those facing higher tax burdens will soon begin to play out in terms of productivity and employment figures, as well as housing sales and business starts. A fair, across-the-board tax code would promote economic growth and broaden the tax base. Don't get me wrong: I hate taxes. But a low tax rate imposed on everyone who works would be preferable to a small minority paying exorbitant amounts for more and more programs—while millions of earners pay nothing at all.

Laying such a big burden on such a small group is bad for democracy; it pits us against one another. George Washington warned in his Farewell Address against instigating partisan resentment that "agitates the community with ill-founded jealousies and false alarms; kindles the animosity of one part against another, foments occasionally riot and insurrection." What happened to Abraham Lincoln's call to rely on "the better angels of our nature"?

## The Growth of Resentment and Entitlement

Just as college kids suddenly become fiscal hawks when they pay their own tuition bills, maybe it's time for more Americans to start paying tax bills. Former White House Press Secretary Ari Fleischer spoke out this week against tax cuts because Americans who earn an income of any size should help shoulder the cost of running our government. Why not give everyone a financial stake in how things turn out? "Given the size of the deficit, fiscal responsibility demands nothing less," Fleischer writes. Here's an opportunity for the president to call on all working Americans to pay some portion, no matter how small, of the cost of our government.

The Obama administration seems perfectly fine with the fact that soon, a majority of Americans will not be paying any federal income tax at all. The class warfare rhetoric coming out of the White House is fueling anger at all levels. It builds hard feelings in those who do pay, and it reinforces the entitlement attitude among those who don't. Feeding resentment is no way to run an economy—or a democracy.

> *"The benefits of extending the upper-income tax cuts . . . will go overwhelmingly to the richest of the rich . . . while costing roughly $1 trillion over the next decade in lost revenue and increased interest costs on the national debt."*

# To Improve US Democracy, End Tax Cuts for the Richest Americans

## Jacob S. Hacker and Paul Pierson

*One of the main issues raised in recent elections has been the increasing US federal budget deficit and the tax cuts that have been singled out by some as a significant cause of this problem. In the viewpoint that follows, Jacob S. Hacker and Paul Pierson advance this view, maintaining that tax cuts for the richest Americans have not only led to the increasing deficit, but have also created a rift in society between wealthy Americans and all other citizens. They argue that this divide has allowed those with money in the country to exert greater control over the election process, which in turn further increases the gap between the rich and everyone else. Closing this gap, Hacker and Pierson conclude, will require reform*

Jacob S. Hacker and Paul Pierson, "For the Good of Democracy, Tax Cuts for the Rich Must Expire," *Los Angeles Times*, September 23, 2010. Used by permission of the author.

*not just of the economy but of the US democratic process. Jacob S. Hacker is a political science professor at Yale, and Paul Pierson is a political science professor at the University of California, Berkeley; they are coauthors of the book* Winner Take All Politics: How Washington Made the Rich Richer—and Turned Its Back on the Middle Class.

As you read, consider the following questions:
1. By how much have the top 400 households' federal income taxes decreased since 1995, as stated by the authors?
2. According to the authors, what is Republicans' argument for continuing tax cuts?
3. According to Rahm Emanuel, as cited by the authors, into what three sections can political campaigns be broken down?

The richest 0.1% of Americans have seen their share of pre-tax national income rise from less than 3% in 1970 to more than 12% in 2007—the highest proportion since the creation of the income tax in 1913. Yet even as the rich grew vastly richer, Washington decided they needed more help. Since 1995, the top 400 households have enjoyed a 45% cut in their federal income taxes (they paid 30% of individual income in 1995 and 16.6% in 2007). In 2007 alone, that saved the top 400 filers $46 million—per household.

In the coming weeks [September 2010], you will hear a great deal of discussion about whether maintaining tax relief for the rich passed in 2001 will create jobs. You will hear much less about the real issue raised by the tax-cut debate: America's fraying democracy.

## Tax Cuts Are Ineffective and Unpopular

Most economists agree that extending Bush-era tax cuts for the highest-income Americans would do little to stimulate the

Republicans vs. Democrats Cartoon; 2011 AOL Inc. Used with permission.

economy. The nonpartisan Congressional Budget Office recently ranked extending the 2001 tax cuts last among 11 options for creating employment. It noted that even within that option, extending tax cuts for the rich would be the least helpful tax-cut extension, because wealthy people would be likely to bank their tax savings rather than spending them.

Good ideas for putting Americans back to work are running into a wall of congressional opposition in the face of deficit worries. Yet the same members of Congress who denounce deficit spending are ready to find vast sums for the idea that ranks dead last.

For a while, pundits chalked this up to election-year pandering. Yet multiple polls have confirmed that by large margins, Americans don't favor keeping the high-end tax cuts. This means politicians are flocking toward a proposal that is at once ineffective and unpopular.

Of course, no one is really surprised by the GOP [Republican] position. Even if jobs were plentiful, Republicans would be insisting on extending all the Bush tax cuts. Budget surplus? Budget deficit? Weak economy? Strong economy? For roughly two decades, the Republican answer has been the same: tax reductions for the most well-off. At times the mantra seemed particularly absurd: Just before the invasion of Iraq, House Majority Leader Tom DeLay told a group of bankers that "nothing is more important in the face of a war than cutting taxes."

Today, the Republicans' main argument is that breaks for those at the top are crucial for small businesses—even though, as House Republican leader John Boehner recently admitted, the overwhelming majority of small-business owners won't be affected. The benefits of extending the upper-income tax cuts instead will go overwhelmingly to the richest of the rich (tax filers making more than $1 million a year will save an average of $128,832 each), while costing roughly $1 trillion over the next decade in lost revenue and increased interest costs on the national debt.

If you wanted to encourage small-business job growth, there are much more cost-effective ways to do so. But that would not advance the Republicans' campaign to lock in the vast top-end tax cuts passed a decade ago.

## Tax Cuts Drive Politics

The roots of that tax-cutting campaign go back more than a generation. In the wake of a major political mobilization of corporate America in the 1970s, the GOP forged a political coalition bringing together anti-government libertarians, social conservatives and powerful business backers. Tax cuts increasingly proved to be the glue of that coalition, feeding into the conservative cause by starving government (at least in theory) while showering very specific largesse on the GOP's deepest-pocketed supporters.

The real puzzle is why Democrats, the putative party of the little guy, offer cover for these top-heavy initiatives. In 2001, and again today, a nontrivial contingent of Democrats has been willing to blur the conflict and hand victory to the tax cutters, proving that gridlock can be overcome when doing so benefits the well-off.

It's hard to remember, but a small but crucial bloc of Democrats that included Sen. Dianne Feinstein was the key to passing the tax cuts in 2001. This time around, 31 House Democrats have written to Speaker Nancy Pelosi to insist on retaining the upper-income cuts. What might be called "Republican-for-a-Day Democrats" are not always moderates in GOP-leaning districts. Charles E. Schumer of New York, for example, has been one of the fiercest defenders of favorable tax treatment for hedge-fund managers, a widely condemned tax loophole benefiting the superrich that still survives four years after the Democratic capture of Congress.

Tax-cutting Democrats sometimes reflect the pull of local economic interests. But they also reflect the post-1980s shift of the party as a whole toward business and affluent donors in an increasingly money-driven political world. During his time directing the campaign efforts of congressional Democrats, Rahm Emanuel, now Obama's chief of staff, reportedly offered this wisdom: "The first third of your campaign is money, money, money. The second third is money, money and press. And the last third is votes, press and money." (For those keeping score at home, that's money 6, votes 1.)

## Democracy Will Close the Economic Gap

There is a widely held view that rising inequality is somehow beyond politics, a natural occurrence driven by global economic forces. The skew of tax cutting toward the rich gives the lie to this fatalistic perspective. From rules shaping chief executive pay to financial deregulation to, yes, tax policy, a political system tilted toward those at the top has greatly widened the gap between the rich and everyone else.

To close that gap and restore broad economic growth, we need to improve our democracy, not just our economy.

> "Our democracy is corrupted when
> some voters think that they won't
> have to pay for the benefits their
> representatives offer them. It is
> corrupted when some voters see
> themselves as victims of exploitation
> by their fellow citizens."

# To Improve US Democracy, Make the Tax Code More Transparent

*Charles Murray*

*In the following viewpoint, Charles Murray explains how the current US tax code fosters confusion among US citizens in all tax brackets. He argues that the system of taxation coupled with political rhetoric and occasionally misleading statistical portrayals of taxation have created discontent and have divided citizens. These circumstances have caused resentment in those who pay large percentages of their wages in income taxes and apathy in those who feel they are not shouldering the financial burden of political decisions, thus weakening the democratic system. Murray calls for*

Charles Murray, "Tax Withholding Is Bad for Democracy," *Wall Street Journal*, 254(37), August 13, 2009. Used by permission of the author.

*a rewriting of the tax code that allows for greater transparency so that all US citizens will be aware of their stake in the government and can join together and take an active role in directing its future. Charles Murray is a resident scholar at the conservative American Enterprise Institute and author of the book* Real Education: Four Simple Truths for Bringing America's Schools Back to Reality.

As you read, consider the following questions:
1. As stated by the author, what is the average tax rate of the bottom 50 percent of Americans who file income taxes?
2. What does Murray suggest should be done to reform the tax code regarding payroll and personal taxes?
3. According to the author, what is the effect of tax withholding?

America is supposed to be a democracy in which we're all in it together. Part of that ethos, which has been so essential to the country in times of crisis, is a common understanding that we all pay a share of the costs. Taxes are an essential ingredient in the civic glue that binds us together.

Our democracy is corrupted when some voters think that they won't have to pay for the benefits their representatives offer them. It is corrupted when some voters see themselves as victims of exploitation by their fellow citizens.

By both standards, American democracy is in trouble. We have the worst of both worlds. The rhetoric of the president tells the public that the rich are not paying their fair share, undermining the common understanding from the bottom up. Meanwhile, the IRS recently released new numbers on who pays how much taxes, and those numbers tell the people at the top that they're being exploited.

## The Tax Code Deforms
## Everyone's Behavior

Let's start with the rich, whom I define as families in the top 1% of income among those who filed tax returns. In 2007, the year with the most recent tax data, they had family incomes of $410,000 or more. They paid 40% of all the personal income taxes collected.

Yes, you read it right: 1% of American families paid 40% of America's personal taxes.

The families in the rest of the top 5% had family incomes of $160,000 to $410,000. They paid another 20% of total personal income taxes. Now we're up to three out of every five dollars in personal taxes paid by just five out of every 100 American families.

Turn to the bottom three-quarters of the families who filed income tax returns in 2007—not just low-income families, but everybody with family incomes below $66,500. That 75% of families paid just 13% of all personal income taxes. Scott Hodge of the Tax Foundation has recast these numbers in terms of a single, stunning statistic: The top 1% of American households pay more in federal taxes than the bottom 95% combined.

My point is not that the rich are being bled dry. The taxes paid by families in the top 1% amounted to 22% of their adjusted gross income, not a confiscatory rate. The issue is that it is inherently problematic to have a democracy in which a third of filers pay no personal income tax at all (another datum from the IRS), and the entire bottom half of filers, meaning those with adjusted gross incomes below $33,000, have an average tax rate of just 3%.

This deforms the behavior of everyone—the voters who think they aren't paying for Congress's latest bright idea, the politicians who know that promising new programs will always be a winning political strategy with the majority of taxpayers who don't think they have to pay for them, and the wealthy who know that the only way to get politicians to refrain from that strategy is to buy them off.

## Tax Code Transparency Is Necessary

For once, we face a problem with a solution that costs nothing. Most families who pay little or no personal income taxes are paying Social Security and Medicare taxes. All we need to do is make an accounting change, no longer pretending that payroll taxes are sequestered in trust funds.

Fold payroll taxes into the personal tax code, adjusting the rules so that everyone still pays the same total, but the tax bill shows up on the 1040. Doing so will tell everyone the truth: Their payroll taxes are being used to pay whatever bills the federal government brings upon itself, among which are the costs of Social Security and Medicare.

The finishing touch is to make sure that people understand how much they are paying, which is presently obscured by withholding at the workplace. End withholding, and require everybody to do what millions of Americans already do: write checks for estimated taxes four times a year.

Both of those simple changes scare politicians. Payroll taxes are politically useful because low-income and middle-income taxpayers don't complain about what they believe are contributions to their retirement and they think, wrongly, that they aren't paying much for anything else. Tax withholding has a wonderfully anesthetizing effect on people whose only income is a paycheck, leaving many of them actually feeling grateful for their tax refund check every year, not noticing how much the government has taken from them.

## Honesty Could Reform Tax Code Problems

But the politicians' fear of being honest about taxes doesn't change the urgent need to be honest. The average taxpayer is wrong if he believes the affluent aren't paying their fair share—

the top income earners carry an extraordinary proportion of the tax burden. High-income earners are wrong, too, about being exploited: Take account of payroll taxes, and low-income people also bear a heavy tax load.

End the payroll tax, end withholding, and these corrosive misapprehensions go away. We will once again be a democracy in which we're all in it together, we all know that we're all paying a share, and we are all aware how much that share is.

> *"[The* Citizens United *opinion] offered*
> *no reason for supposing that allowing*
> *rich corporations to swamp elections*
> *with money will . . . produce a better-*
> *informed public—and there are many*
> *reasons to think it will produce a*
> *worse-informed one."*

# Corporate Funding of Political Ads Will Hinder the Democratic Election Process

*Ronald Dworkin*

*In January 2010, the US Supreme Court handed down a ruling in the case* Citizens United v. Federal Election Commission (FEC) *that allows corporate entities to spend as much money as they desire to produce political broadcasts. Ronald Dworkin argues in the following viewpoint that allowing corporations free reign to spend as much money as they deem fit in support of or opposition to a particular issue or candidate will damage the US democratic election process. He worries that this lack of limitation will mislead and misinform the public and will allow corporations to wield excessive influence over the outcome of elections. Ronald Dworkin is a professor of law and philosophy at New York University and*

*University College London and the author of the book* Is Democracy Possible Here?

As you read, consider the following questions:
1. What are some of the legislation and court decisions mentioned by the author as precedents overturned with the *Citizens United* decision?
2. According to the author, in what ways will corporate advertising mislead and misinform the public?
3. What evidence does the author present to support his claim that the *Citizens United* decision will encourage corruption?

No Supreme Court decision in decades has generated such open hostilities among the three branches of our government as has the Court's 5-4 decision in *Citizens United v. FEC* [Federal Election Commission] in January 2010. The five conservative justices, on their own initiative, at the request of no party to the suit, declared that corporations and unions have a constitutional right to spend as much as they wish on television election commercials specifically supporting or targeting particular candidates. President Obama immediately denounced the decision as a catastrophe for American democracy and then, in a highly unusual act, repeated his denunciation in his State of the Union address with six of the justices sitting before him. . . .

The history of the Court's decision is as extraordinary as its reception. At least since 1907, when Congress passed the Tillman Act at the request of President Theodore Roosevelt, it had been accepted by the nation and the Court that corporations, which are only fictitious persons created by law, do not have the same First Amendment rights to political activity as real people do. In 1990, in *Austin v. Michigan Chamber of Commerce*, the Court firmly upheld that principle. In 2002, Congress passed the Bipartisan

Campaign Reform Act (BCRA) sponsored by Senators John McCain and Russell Feingold, which forbade corporations to engage in television electioneering for a period of thirty days before a primary for federal office and sixty days before an election. In 2003, in *McConnell v. Federal Election Commission (FEC)*, the Court upheld the constitutionality of that prohibition.

## A Ruling Damaging to Democracy

In the 2008 presidential primary season a small corporation, Citizens United, financed to a minor extent by corporate contributions, tried to broadcast a derogatory movie about Hillary Clinton. The FEC declared the broadcast illegal under the BCRA. Citizens United then asked the Supreme Court to declare it exempt from that statute on the ground, among others, that it proposed to broadcast its movie only on a pay-per-view channel. It did not challenge the constitutionality of the act. But the five conservative justices—Chief Justice [John] Roberts and Justices Samuel Alito, Anthony Kennedy, Antonin Scalia, and Clarence Thomas—decided on their own initiative, after a rehearing they themselves called for, that they wanted to declare the act unconstitutional anyway.

They said that the BCRA violated the First Amendment, which declares that Congress shall make no law infringing the freedom of speech. They agreed that their decision was contrary to the *Austin* and *McConnell* precedents; they therefore overruled those decisions as well as repealing a century of American history and tradition. Their decision threatens an avalanche of negative political commercials financed by huge corporate wealth, beginning in this year's [2010] midterm elections. Overall these commercials can be expected to benefit Republican candidates and to injure candidates whose records dissatisfy powerful industries. The decision gives corporate lobbyists, already much too influential in our political system, an immensely powerful weapon. It is important to study in some detail a ruling so damaging to democracy.

## Responsible Adjudication Depends on Careful Interpretation

The First Amendment, like many of the Constitution's most important provisions, is drafted in the abstract language of political morality: it guarantees a "right" of free speech but does not specify the dimensions of that right—whether it includes a right of cigarette manufacturers to advertise their product on television, for instance, or a right of a Ku Klux Klan chapter publicly to insult and defame blacks or Jews, or a right of foreign governments to broadcast political advice in American elections. Decisions on these and a hundred other issues require interpretation and if any justice's interpretation is not to be arbitrary or purely partisan, it must be guided by principle—by some theory of why speech deserves exemption from government regulation in principle. Otherwise the Constitution's language becomes only a meaningless mantra to be incanted whenever a judge wants for any reason to protect some form of communication. Precedent—how the First Amendment has been interpreted and applied by the Supreme Court in the past—must also be respected. But since the meaning of past decisions is also a matter of interpretation, that, too, must be guided by a principled account of the First Amendment's point.

A First Amendment theory is therefore indispensible to responsible adjudication of free speech issues. Many such theories have been offered by justices, lawyers, constitutional scholars, and philosophers, and most of them assign particular importance to the protection of political speech—speech about candidates for public office and about issues that are or might be topics of partisan political debate. But none of these theories—absolutely none of them—justifies the damage the five conservative justices have just inflicted on our politics.

## Corporate Advertising Would Not Inform the Electorate

The most popular of these theories appeals to the need for an informed electorate. Freedom of political speech is an essential condition of an effective democracy because it ensures that voters have access to as wide and diverse a range of information and political opinion as possible. Oliver Wendell Holmes Jr., Learned Hand, and other great judges and scholars argued that citizens are more likely to reach good decisions if no ideas, however radical, are censored. But even if that is not so, the basic justification of majoritarian democracy—that it gives power to the informed and settled opinions of the largest number of people—nevertheless requires what Holmes called a "free marketplace of ideas."

Kennedy, who wrote the Court's opinion in *Citizens United* on behalf of the five conservatives, appealed to the "informed electorate" theory. But he offered no reason for supposing that allowing rich corporations to swamp elections with money will in fact produce a better-informed public—and there are many reasons to think it will produce a worse-informed one. Corporations have no ideas of their own. Their ads will promote the opinions of their managers, who could publish or broadcast those opinions on their own or with others of like mind through political action committees (PACs) or other organizations financed through voluntary individual contributions. So though allowing them to use their stockholders' money rather than their own will increase the volume of advertising, it will not add to the diversity of ideas offered to voters.

Corporate advertising will mislead the public, moreover, because its volume will suggest more public support than there actually is for the opinions the ads express. Many of the shareholders who will actually pay for the ads, who in many cases are members of pension and union funds, will hate the opinions they pay to advertise. Obama raised a great deal of money on the Internet, mostly from small contributors, to finance his presidential campaign, and we can expect political parties, candidates, and PACs to tap that source much more effectively in the future. But these contributions are made voluntarily by supporters, not by managers using the money of people who may well be opposed to their opinions. Corporate advertising is misleading in another way as well. It purports to offer opinions about the public interest, but in fact managers are legally required to spend corporate funds only to promote their corporation's own financial interests, which may very well be different.

## Monopolies Destroy the Marketplace of Ideas

There is, however, a much more important flaw in the conservative justices' argument. If corporations exercise the power that the Court has now given them, and buy an extremely large share of the television time available for political ads, their electioneering will undermine rather than improve the public's political education. Kennedy declared that speech may not be restricted just to make candidates more equal in their financial resources. But he misunderstood why other nations limit campaign expenditures. This is not just to be fair to all candidates, like requiring a single starting line for runners in a race, but to create the best conditions for the public to make an informed decision when it votes—the main purpose of the First Amendment, according to the marketplace theory. The Supreme Court of Canada understands the difference between these different goals. Creating "a level playing field for those who wish to engage in the electoral discourse," it said, "enables voters to be better informed; no one voice is overwhelmed by another."

Monopolies and near monopolies are just as destructive to the marketplace of ideas as they are to any other market. A public debate about climate change, for instance, would not do much to improve the understanding of its audience if speaking time were auctioned so that energy companies were able to buy vastly more time than academic scientists. The great mass of voters is already very much more aware of electoral advertising spots constantly repeated, like beer ads, in popular dramatic series or major sports telecasts than of opinions reported mainly on public broadcasting news programs. Unlimited corporate advertising will make that distortion much greater.

## Corporations' Economic Advantage After *Citizens United*

What functional difference does *Citizens United* achieve by permitting corporations to spend treasury funds on independent expenditures? A key difference is that shareholders obtain the advantage of streamlined aggregation through the corporation, as opposed to other entities. For non-shareholders to aggregate their money, they must pool funds, subject to personal income tax, by contributing individually to a PAC [political action committee] or political party. The PAC or party collects their pooled money, but it does so only subject to applicable restrictions on contributions under campaign finance law. By contrast, the post–*Citizens United* corporation may serve as both a source of funds and the pooling entity for those funds all at once for its shareholders. It can pool shareholder money simply by retaining earnings, instead of distributing dividends to shareholders who would then need to aggregate those funds through a separate entity. This streamlined aggregation not only lowers transaction costs, but also uses pre-tax dollars (for purposes of personal income tax) and bypasses restrictions on contributions. Aggregation through PACs and parties is quite inefficient by comparison. It is therefore difficult to understand why shareholders should be constitutionally entitled to this advantage.

*Michael S. Kang, "After* Citizens United,*"*
Indiana Law Review, *vol. 44, no. 2, 2010.*

The difference between the two goals I distinguished—aiming at electoral equality for its own sake and reducing inequality in order to protect the integrity of political debate—is real and important. If a nation capped permissible electoral expenditure at

a very low level, it would achieve the greatest possible financial equality. But it would damage the quality of political debate by not permitting enough discussion and by preventing advocates of novel or unfamiliar opinion from spending enough funds to attract any public attention. Delicate judgment is needed to determine how much inequality must be permitted in order to ensure robust debate and an informed population. But allowing corporations to spend their corporate treasure on television ads conspicuously fails that test. Judged from the perspective of this theory of the First Amendment's purpose—that it aims at a better-educated populace—the conservatives' decision is all loss and no gain.

## Corporations Do Not Have Emotions

A second popular theory focuses on the importance of free speech not to educate the public at large but to protect the status, dignity, and moral development of individual citizens as equal partners in the political process. Justice John Paul Stevens summarized this theory in the course of his very long but irresistibly powerful dissenting opinion in *Citizens United*. Speaking for himself and Justices Stephen Breyer, Ruth Ginsburg, and Sonia Sotomayor, he said that "one fundamental concern of the First Amendment is to 'protec[t] the individual's interest in self-expression.'" Kennedy tried to appeal to this understanding of the First Amendment to justify free speech for corporations. "By taking the right to speak from some and giving it to others," he stated, "the Government deprives the disadvantaged person or class of the right to use speech to strive to establish worth, standing, and respect for the speaker's voice." But this is bizarre. The interests the First Amendment protects, on this second theory, are only the moral interests of individuals who would suffer frustration and indignity if they were censored. Only real human beings can have those emotions or suffer those insults. Corporations, which are only artificial legal inventions, cannot. The right to vote is surely at least as important a badge of equal citizenship

as the right to speak, but not even the conservative justices have suggested that every corporation should have a ballot.

## Corporations Could Influence Congressmen

A third widely accepted purpose of the First Amendment lies in its contribution to honesty and transparency in government. If government were free to censor its critics, or to curtail the right to a free press guaranteed in a separate phrase of the First Amendment, then it would be harder for the public to discover official corruption. The Court's *Citizens United* decision does nothing to serve that further purpose. Corporations do not need to run television ads in the run-up to an election urging votes against particular candidates in order to report discoveries they may make about official dishonesty, or in order to defend themselves against any accusation of dishonesty made against them. And of course they have everyone else's access to print and television reporters.

Though the Court's decision will do nothing to deter corruption in that way, it will do a great deal to encourage one particularly dangerous form of it. It will sharply increase the opportunity of corporations to tempt or intimidate congressmen facing reelection campaigns. Obama and Speaker Nancy Pelosi had great difficulty persuading some members of the House of Representatives to vote for the health care reform bill, which finally passed with a dangerously thin majority, because those members feared they were risking their seats in the coming midterm elections. They knew, after the Court's decision, that they might face not just another party and candidate but a tidal wave of negative ads financed by health insurance companies with enormous sums of their shareholders' money to spend.

## Corporate Influence Was Previously Rampant

Kennedy wrote that there is no substantial risk of such corrupting influence so long as corporations do not "coordinate" their electioneering with any candidate's formal campaign. That seems particularly naive. Few congressmen would be unaware of or indifferent to the likelihood of a heavily financed advertising campaign urging voters to vote for him, if he worked in a corporation's interests, or against him if he did not. No coordination—no role of any candidate or his agents in the design of the ads—would be necessary.

Kennedy's naiveté seems even stranger when we notice the very substantial record of undue corporate influence laid before Congress when it adopted the BCRA. Before that act, corporations and other organizations were free to broadcast "issue" ads that did not explicitly endorse or oppose any candidates. The district court judge who first heard the *Citizens United* case found that, according to testimony of lobbyists and political consultants, at least some "Members of Congress are particularly grateful when negative issue advertisements are run by these organizations. . .[that]. . .use issue advocacy as a means to influence various Members of Congress." That influence can be expected to be even greater now that the Court has permitted explicit political endorsements or opposition as well. Kennedy's optimism went further: he denied that heavy corporate spending would lead the public to suspect that form of corruption. But the district court judge had reported that:

> 80 percent of Americans polled are of the view that corporations and other organizations that engage in electioneering communications, which benefit specific elected officials, receive special consideration from those officials when matters arise that affect these corporations and organizations. . . .

The Supreme Court's conservative phalanx has demonstrated once again its power and will to reverse America's drive to greater equality and more genuine democracy. It threatens a step-by-step return to a constitutional stone age of right-wing ideology. Once again it offers justifications that are untenable in both constitutional theory and legal precedent. Stevens's remarkable dissent in this case shows how much we will lose when he soon retires. We must hope that Obama nominates a progressive replacement who not only is young enough to endure the bad days ahead but has enough intellectual firepower to help construct a rival and more attractive vision of what our Constitution really means.

> *"Speech is an essential mechanism of democracy and the means to hold officials accountable to the people. As such, political speech must prevail against laws that would suppress it."*

# Corporate Funding of Political Ads Will Not Hinder the Democratic Election Process

*Hans A. von Spakovsky*

*Following the decision in the Supreme Court case* Citizens United v. Federal Election Commission, *critics charged that the ruling would allow corporations and special interests to hijack elections by providing huge amounts of cash reserves to particular candidates. However, advocates of the decision contend that it was a just and necessary means of upholding the First Amendment right to free speech. Hans A. von Spakovsky takes this stance in the following viewpoint, arguing that the Supreme Court ruling is important because it has given a voice to all entities in the political process. He further maintains that many critiques of the ruling— including fears that foreign corporations will be able to invest in elections—are unfounded or reveal partisan politicking. Hans A. von Spakovsky is a senior legal fellow at the Heritage Foundation's*

Hans von Spakovsky, "Citizens United and the Restoration of the First Amendment," *Heritage Legal Memorandum #50*, February 17, 2010. Used by permission of Heritage Foundation.

*Center for Legal and Judicial Studies and formerly served on the Federal Election Commission.*

As you read, consider the following questions:
1. As stated by the author, what entities in addition to corporations are now allowed to spend freely on political broadcasts?
2. From what types of political involvement does the author claim foreign nationals are banned?
3. How are union members' rights and views more at risk than shareholders' in light of the *Citizens United* decision, according to the author?

In the Supreme Court's landmark decision in *Citizens United v. Federal Election Commission*, Justice Anthony Kennedy and a majority of the Court upheld some of this nation's most important founding principles: the right to engage in free speech—particularly political speech—and the right to freely associate. Although corporations and unions still cannot contribute directly to political candidates, the Court overturned a federal ban on independent political advocacy by corporations and unions.

Critics of this holding, including President Barack Obama, claim that the decision will "open the floodgates for special interests—including foreign corporations—to spend without limit in our elections" and that shareholders must be protected from political expenditures by corporations in which they own shares. Neither of these criticisms is justified. Foreign nationals, including foreign corporations, are banned from participating directly or indirectly in American elections by federal statute and Federal Election Commission (FEC) regulations. The *Citizens United* decision did not even consider that ban, let alone overturn it.

Corporate shareholders can already influence the behavior of the corporations in which they own shares through shareholder votes. Moreover, they can vote with their feet by selling their stock and moving on to another company if they disapprove of their corporation's activities.

What is most telling about critics' supposed concern for shareholders' rights, however, is their lack of any parallel concern for union members. Unlike shareholders who can walk out on any company they do not like, many union members cannot simply cancel their membership if they are unhappy with the political expenditure of millions of dollars by their union leadership.

## Previous Legislation Limited Free Speech

Citizens United (CU) is a nonprofit corporation that produced a documentary, *Hillary: The Movie*, that was critical of then-Senator Hillary Clinton when she was a presidential candidate in January 2008. The movie was released in theaters and on DVD, and CU wanted to make it available through video-on-demand to cable subscribers. CU produced several advertisements that it intended to run on broadcast and cable television to promote the film.

As a nonprofit corporation, however, CU was prohibited under the challenged provision from using its general treasury funds to make independent expenditures for political speech defined as an "electioneering communication" or for speech expressly advocating the election or defeat of a candidate for federal office. Pursuant to the challenged statute, such expenditures could be made only through a separate segregated fund or political action committee (PAC) established by the corporation or union that used funds voluntarily donated by stockholders and the executive and administrative personnel of a corporation or the members of a union.

Not only did this ban apply to for-profit corporations, but it also applied to many nonprofit associations on both sides of the political aisle, from the NAACP [National Association for the Advancement of Colored People] to the Sierra Club to the

National Rifle Association, almost all of which are also corporations. Under penalty of criminal and civil sanctions, those corporate associations were prohibited from expressing their members' views with respect to which particular candidates should be elected to uphold favorable positions on important public policy issues unless they established a separate PAC or could qualify as a Massachusetts Citizens for Life (MCFL)–type corporation, defined as an ideological nonprofit organization that does not accept corporate or labor contributions. The provisions governing PACs and MCFL corporations are so onerous that the Court concluded that they "function as the equivalent of prior restraint" on speech.

## The Decision Overturned Unconstitutional Bans

The Court threw out the federal ban on independent political advocacy by corporations (and, thus, labor unions and national banks) by overturning its prior decision in *Austin v. Michigan State Chamber of Commerce*, which had upheld a state ban on independent expenditures by a nonprofit trade association. The Court also overturned part of *McConnell v. FEC*, which had upheld the "electioneering communications" provision that was added to federal law in 2002 as part of the McCain-Feingold law [for campaign finance reform].

Banning independent political advocacy violates the First Amendment because it effectively limits speech. The Court rejected the idea that the government can decide who gets to speak and that the government can actually impose "federal felony punishment" on some for speaking at all, particularly those who speak through associations of members who share their beliefs.

The Court held that the First Amendment stands against attempts to distinguish among different speakers, which "are all too often simply a means to control content." In so doing, the Court correctly held that the government cannot impose restrictions on certain disfavored speakers such as corporations.

The Court also found that First Amendment free speech rights do not depend on a speaker's financial ability to engage in public discussion: The fact that some speakers may have more wealth than others does not diminish their First Amendment rights.

Finally, independent advertisements and expenditures, including "those made by corporations, do not give rise to corruption or the appearance of corruption," the basis for upholding other campaign finance restrictions. Speech is an essential mechanism of democracy and the means to hold officials accountable to the people. As such, political speech must prevail against laws that would suppress it.

## Regulations Prevent the Participation of Foreign Corporations

The claim that foreign corporations will now be able to spend money to influence federal elections is completely false, and there is no need for further legislation on this issue. Federal law bans all foreign nationals from contributing either directly or indirectly to any candidate or political party "in connection with a Federal, State, or local election." It also bans all foreign nationals from making "an expenditure, independent expenditure, or disbursement for an electioneering communication."

Thus, foreign nationals are banned not only from contributing directly to candidates, but also from making any political expenditures of any kind. This ban includes foreign corporations, since the term "foreign nationals" is defined to include individuals, foreign governments, foreign political parties, and corporations "organized under the laws or having [their] principal place of business in a foreign country." The punishment for violating this provision can be severe: In addition to civil penalties, knowing and willful violations that aggregate $2,000 or more in a calendar year can result in up to one year in federal prison, and violations aggregating $25,000 or more can result in up to five years in federal prison.

There is an exemption for foreign nationals who are lawful permanent residents of the United States. The FEC has implemented congressional intent in this exemption with regard to corporations by issuing regulations that allow only American domestic subsidiaries of foreign corporations, not the foreign corporations themselves, to establish PACs. The regulation specifically provides that a "foreign national shall not direct, dictate, control, or directly or indirectly participate in the decision-making process of any person, such as a corporation, labor organization, political committee, or political organization with regard to such person's Federal or non-Federal election-related activities." Such PACs can operate only if their donations and disbursements do "not come from a foreign national" and "no foreign national participates in making decisions" on the PAC's election-related activities. Under current law, there are multiple layers of protection to prevent foreign influence on U.S. elections.

This exemption makes perfect sense. Foreign corporations are prohibited from participating in American elections, but their American subsidiaries that employ American workers, have American officers, and pay American taxes are able to participate in the American election process to the same extent as other companies as long as all of the money comes from, and all of the decisions are made by, Americans.

## Regulation Could Unfairly Restrict Americans' Democratic Participation

It is critical to note that the Court did not even review this ban on foreign nationals, specifically saying that it was not considering "the question whether the Government has a compelling interest in preventing foreign individuals or associations from influencing our Nation's political process." So the claim made by President Obama and others that foreign corporations will be able to spend without limit in U.S. elections is incorrect. The ban on direct contributions and independent expenditures by foreign corporations still stands.

## *Citizens United* Could Be Used to Fight Corruption

On the day when *Citizens United* came down, many scholars and advocates of campaign finance reform condemned it as a "political tsunami" launched by an "activist court." Others doubted the extent of its practical influence. What is clear is that the decision fundamentally changed the terrain of campaign finance—and as that new terrain settles from its present state of flux, legislators have already begun to shape its features.

[It is suggested] that they set their sights on a different path, not only reinforcing disclosure and disclaimer regulations within the previously regulated sphere but expanding those regulations beyond direct candidate advocacy to a broader range of corporate political speech. That approach not only would be constitutionally legitimate; it also might turn out to be more effective than the pre–*Citizens United* regime in informing the electorate, preventing corruption or the appearance of corruption, and protecting shareholders.

> *Daniel Winik, "Citizens Informed:*
> *Disclosure and Disclaimer for Corporate*
> *Electoral Advocacy in the Wake of* Citizens
> United," *Yale Law Journal, vol. 120, no. 3,*
> *December 2010.*

The proposal released by Senator Charles Schumer (D-NY) and Representative Chris Van Hollen (D-MD) on February 11, which would ban corporations from spending money on U.S. elections if they have foreign ownership of more than 20 percent, presents a serious constitutional problem. Since domestic subsidiaries of foreign corporations are already restricted from participating in U.S. elections unless all of the decision making on such expenditures is made by American nationals and all of the funding is generated in the United States, adding a foreign shareholder restriction for all domestic corporations would "only restrict the rights of U.S. nationals to associate for political involvement because of a non-controlling foreign shareholder." Thus, in direct conflict with the *Citizens United* decision, the political speech of certain Americans (not foreigners) would be restricted.

It should be noted that while foreign shareholders are deemed to be a threat, apparently foreign union members are not. Indeed, there are U.S.-based unions with foreign members, including most prominently the Service Employees International Union, which claims it is "the fastest growing union in North America"—including its members in Canada. And there are many nonprofit organizations like Greenpeace with non-U.S. members who apparently raise no concerns with Members of Congress since they are nowhere mentioned in any of these proposals.

## Shareholders Do Not Need Protection

The claim that shareholders of corporations must be "protected" from political expenditures with which they do not agree is equally baseless. The various proposals that are being made to "protect" shareholders are epitomized by a Brennan Center report recommending that federal law be changed to require that corporations obtain the consent of shareholders before making political expenditures and that corporate directors be held *personally liable* for violating this requirement. Supposedly, this "will empower shareholders to affect how their money is spent. It also may preserve more corporate assets by limiting the spending of corporate money on political expenditures."

The first priority of all business corporations is to sell their goods and services and make a profit. It is highly likely that most businesses will avoid what may be perceived as partisan political activities that could upset their customers and hurt their sales.

Corporations may very well speak about government regulations that affect their bottom line, but they *should* also have the ability to speak when government actions threaten to damage their business and the employment prospects of their employees.

Beyond that, why would the average shareholder want to direct corporate management through specific consent requirements for some expenditures but not for others? Many companies also make charitable donations that shareholders may not favor. In fact, corporate giants like Bank of America, Morgan Chase, and Citigroup infamously donated millions of dollars to ACORN, an organization whose corruption is now legendary. None of the critics of the *Citizens United* decision seem interested in ensuring that shareholders give their permission before these types of charitable donations are made.

*All* expenditures made by a corporation can affect its assets, yet there are no proposals to require specific shareholder consent for other types of expenditures. The vast majority of shareholders probably do not want the time-consuming responsibility of approving all of the different types of expenditures made by their companies and also know that shareholder surveys and votes can be very expensive, thereby diminishing corporate assets. If shareholders do want a say in such expenditures, as the Court noted, there is "little evidence of abuse that cannot be corrected by shareholders 'through the procedures of corporate democracy.'"

## Union Members May Not Agree with Leadership Decisions

Moreover, what is especially revealing about these proposals and the supposed deep concern over shareholders' rights is the lack of concern for union members who face a much more difficult dilemma than shareholders. The Brennan Center's 40-page report contains no mention of any need to similarly protect union members. There is apparently no concern whatsoever about empowering union members "to affect how their money is spent."

Despite the tens of millions of dollars individual unions have spent in recent years on political activities, there is also apparently no concern about preserving union "assets by limiting the spending of [union] money on political expenditures." Unlike shareholders who can sell the stock of any company they do not like, many union members cannot simply cancel their membership. Indeed, less than half of the states have right-to-work laws under which workers cannot be forced to join a union. Employees in some national industries like the airline and railway industries are also not protected by right-to-work laws.

Union members do have certain rights under the Supreme Court's decision in *Communication Workers v. Beck*, but those rights do not include the right to vote on each ad funded by their union. Unions cannot force members to pay the portion of their union dues that would be used for political purposes, but this right is notoriously difficult to enforce by union members that want to opt out of such political expenditures and falls far short of what is being sought for shareholders. For example, there is no secret ballot; union members must publicly declare to the union leadership that they want to exercise their *Beck* rights. It is also an all-or-nothing proposal; union members cannot object on a case-by-case basis to specific political expenditures that the union leadership wants to make on particular candidates or issues.

Many unions also deliberately make it very difficult for members to exercise these rights, working actively to frustrate and delay compliance, and there is considerable evidence of coercion, threats, ostracism, and abuse of union members who try to opt out. There is a clear dichotomy between the views of union members and their leadership. This is dramatically demonstrated by the fact that "almost two in five union members [of the AFSCME [American Federation of State, County, and Municipal Employees] and the AFL-CIO [American Federation of Labor and Congress of Industrial Organizations]] voted for President George W. Bush in the 2004 election, [yet] both these unions gave over 97 percent of their donations to Democratic candidates." Thus, it is really union members, not corporate shareholders, who are much more in need of a federal law that would force their leaders to get the approval of their members (by secret ballot to avoid intimidation) before making any political expenditures. . . .

## Criticism of *Citizens United* Stems from Partisan Politics

Given that federal law and regulations already ban foreign corporations from participating in American elections, either directly through contributions or indirectly through independent political expenditures, there is no need for further legislation. Some of the proposals being made to restrict domestic corporations that have foreign shareholders also raise other constitutional concerns.

Given the obvious lack of consistency in the claims being advanced on behalf of shareholders and the pointed exclusion of unions and nonprofit associations, it seems clear that these proposals for shareholder "rights" are best suited to the advancement of partisan politics rather than the actual rights of shareholders. There is no need for legislation on behalf of shareholders who are already protected through the shareholder voting process and who can sell the shares of companies whose policies they dislike. All of these concerns are, to borrow from Shakespeare, much ado about nothing.

# Periodical Bibliography

*The following articles have been selected to supplement the diverse views presented in this chapter.*

Jan Witold Baran — "Stampede Toward Democracy," *New York Times*, January 26, 2010.

Yasmin Dawood — "The New Inequality: Constitutional Democracy and the Problem of Wealth," *Maryland Law Review*, 2007.

Kristen M. Formanek — "There's 'No Such Thing as Too Much Speech': How Advertising Deregulation and the Marketplace of Ideas Can Protect Democracy in America," *Iowa Law Review*, July 1, 2009.

Tom Fox — "When Politics Become Frozen," *National Catholic Reporter*, October 15, 2010.

David Graeber — "Value, Politics and Democracy in the United States," *Current Sociology*, March 1, 2011.

Peter Hannaford — "Why Should Liberals Fear Court's McCain-Feingold Decision?," *Human Events*, February 1, 2010.

Sara Jerome — "New Rules on Ad Spots?," *National Journal*, February 13, 2010.

John B. Judis — "Neutralized," *New Republic*, April 28, 2011.

Michael J. Malbin — "Expand Democracy," *American Interest*, July-August 2010.

Robert B. Reich — "What Happened to Democracy?," *American Prospect*, March 2010.

OPPOSING
VIEWPOINTS®
SERIES

CHAPTER 4

# Should the United States Foster Democracy Worldwide?

# Chapter Preface

During his two terms as president of the United States, George W. Bush's foreign policy strategies became collectively known as the Bush Doctrine. While this term was not an official title given to the set of policies implemented by the administration, it became the commonly used phrase to describe the range of foreign policy actions undertaken by the president in the name of national security and defense. One of the main tenets of this doctrine was the spreading of democracy around the world as a way to ensure US security and international stability. The reasoning behind this strategy stemmed from the belief that foreign governments, particularly those in the Middle East, that harbored terrorists and presented a threat to the United States did so because they were totalitarian and the people did not have a say in their governance. Furthermore, this logic maintained that if the people of these countries experienced the freedom that came with democracy, they would no longer tolerate the type of despotism that seemed a breeding ground for terrorism.

Throughout Bush's presidency, this strategy of democracy promotion as both foreign policy and national security strategy was harshly criticized by some commentators who saw it as a misguided and wrongheaded pursuit that would create new problems while solving none. Writing in *Foreign Policy* in September/October 2004, Eric Hobsbawm denounced the effort to spread democracy as "dangerous." He went on to explain his misgivings about the policy, stating, "This rhetoric surrounding this crusade implies that the system is applicable in a standardized (Western) form, that it can succeed everywhere, that it can remedy today's transnational dilemmas, and that it can bring peace, rather than sow disorder. It cannot." Critiques such as these persisted throughout Bush's presidency even as what appeared to be tangible changes in the Middle East began to develop during his second term.

While critics saw the Bush Doctrine as disastrous, others lauded it as courageous and identified it as the needed catalyst for change in the Middle East. Following the establishment of free elections in parts of the Middle East in 2005, Charles Krauthammer praised the Bush Doctrine in the pages of *Time* magazine in March of that year, crediting Bush's active spreading of democracy as the beacon of hope that drove people across the region—in Iraq, Afghanistan, Egypt, and Lebanon—to peacefully participate in elections, express their dissatisfaction with tyranny, and rise up against dictators. He writes of the elections, "It was not people power that set this in motion. It was American power. People power followed." From this point of view, democratic change in the region resulted directly from the Bush Doctrine's pursuit to spread democracy worldwide.

While the Bush Doctrine is no longer the official policy of the United States as its founder has since left office and been succeeded by Barack Obama, the repercussions of the policy to spread democracy continue to have lasting effects on society and foreign policy today. With populist uprisings taking hold across the Middle East at the close of 2010 and throughout the first half of 2011, the role of the United States in fostering democracy in this region and around the world remains a point of contention. The authors in the following chapter debate the issue of democracy promotion, focusing on its impact on national security, US involvement in Middle East democratic uprisings, and the creation of a "league of democracies."

*"Despite all its bad press, democracy promotion remains, in the long run, the most effective way to undermine terrorism and political violence in the Middle East."*

# Promoting Democracy Worldwide Increases US National Security

**Shadi Hamid and Steven Brooke**

*Following the September 11, 2001, terrorist attacks against the United States, the George W. Bush administration instituted a policy of democracy promotion in the Middle East as a method to combat terrorism. Critics have claimed that in the nearly ten years since its inception, this policy has lost much support. However, in the viewpoint that follows, Shadi Hamid and Steven Brooke argue that democracy promotion in the Middle East remains one of the most important policy steps the United States can take to stop terrorism. They contend that the Bush administration's policy failed not because it was a bad policy, but because it was never implemented completely or with enough support to achieve genuine, lasting results. Hamid and Brooke cite studies conducted in the intervening years that show that where democracy is absent,*

Shadi Hamid and Steven Brooke, "Promoting Democracy to Stop Terror, Revisited," *Policy Review*, vol. 159, February/March, 2010. All rights reserved. Reproduced by permission.

*terrorism takes hold. Shadi Hamid is the director of research at the Brookings Doha Center, a project of the Saban Center for Middle East Policy at the Brookings Institution. Steven Brooke is a PhD student in the Department of Government at the University of Texas at Austin.*

As you read, consider the following questions:

1. How did democracy promotion in the Middle East develop as a policy following the September 11 attacks, as described by the authors?
2. As stated by the authors, what are the nationalities of the largest percentages of al Qaeda fighters in Iraq?
3. What do the authors believe to be the domestic political consequences resulting from the connection between lack of democracy and terrorism?

U.S. democracy promotion in the Middle East has suffered a series of crippling defeats. Despite occasionally paying lip service to the idea, few politicians on either the left or right appear committed to supporting democratic reform as a central component of American policy in the region. Who can really blame them, given that democracy promotion has become toxic to a public with little patience left for various "missions" abroad? But as the Obama administration struggles to renew ties with the Muslim world, particularly in light of the June 2009 Cairo speech, it should resist the urge to abandon its predecessor's focus on promoting democracy in what remains the most undemocratic region in the world.

Promoting democratic reform, this time not just with rhetoric but with action, should be given higher priority in the current administration, even though early indications suggest the opposite may be happening. Despite all its bad press, democracy promotion remains, in the long run, the most effective way to undermine terrorism and political violence in the Middle East.

This is not a very popular argument. Indeed, a key feature of the post–[George W.] Bush debate over democratization is an insistence on separating support for democracy from any explicit national security rationale. This, however, would be a mistake with troubling consequences for American foreign policy.

## Abandoning Democracy Promotion Is a Mistake

The twilight of the Bush presidency and the start of Obama's ushered in an expansive discussion over the place of human rights and democracy in American foreign policy. An emerging consensus suggests that the U.S. approach must be fundamentally reassessed and "repositioned." This means, in part, a scaling down of scope and ambition and of avoiding the sweeping Wilsonian tones of recent years. That certainly sounds good. Anything, after all, would be better than the Bush administration's disconcerting mix of revolutionary pro-democracy rhetoric with time-honored realist policies of privileging "stable" pro-American dictators. This only managed to wring the worst out of both approaches.

For its part, the Obama administration has made a strategic decision to shift the focus to resolving the Israeli-Palestinian conflict, which it sees, correctly, as a major source of Arab grievance. This, in turn, has led the administration to strengthen ties with autocratic regimes, such as Egypt and Jordan, which it sees as critical to the peace process.

Some might see such developments as a welcome re-prioritization. However, by downgrading support of Middle East democracy to one among many policy priorities, we risk returning to a pre-9/11 status quo, where the promotion of democracy would neither be worn on our sleeve nor trump short-term hard interests. The "transformative" nature of any democracy promotion project would be replaced by a more sober, targeted focus on providing technical assistance to legislative and judicial branches and strengthening civil society organizations in the region. In many ways, this would be a welcome change from the ideological overload of the post-9/11 environment. But in other ways, it would not.

Those who wish to avoid a piecemeal approach to reform and revive U.S. efforts to support democracy often come back to invocations of American exceptionalism and the argument that the United States, as the world's most powerful nation, has a responsibility to advance the very ideals which animated its founding. These arguments are attractive and admirable, but how durable can they be when translated into concrete policy initiatives? In the wake of a war ostensibly waged in the name of democracy, can a strategy resting on gauzy moral imperatives garner bipartisan support and therefore long-term policy stability? In an ideal world, there would not be a need to justify or rationalize supporting democracy abroad; the moral imperative would be enough. But in the world of politics and decision-making, it rarely is.

## Democracy Promotion Was a Rhetorical Device

After the attacks of September 11th, a basic, intuitive proposition surfaced—that without basic democratic freedoms, citizens lack peaceful, constructive means to express their grievances and are thus more likely to resort to violence. Accordingly, 9/11 did not happen because the terrorists hated our freedom, but, rather, because the Middle East's stifling political environment had bred frustration, anger, and, ultimately, violence. Many in the region saw us as complicit, in large part because we were actively supporting—to the tune of billions of dollars in economic and military aid—the region's most repressive regimes. The realization that our longstanding support of dictatorships had backfired, producing a Middle East rife with instability and political violence, was a sobering one, and grounded the policy debate in a way that has since been lost. The unfolding debate was interesting to watch, if only because it contradicted the popular perception that Republicans were uninterested in the "root causes" of terrorism. In fact, they were. And their somewhat novel ideas on how to address them would begin to figure prominently in the rhetoric and policies of the Bush administration.

In a landmark speech at the National Endowment for Democracy in November 2003, President Bush argued that "as long as the Middle East remains a place where freedom does not flourish, it will remain a place of stagnation, resentment, and violence ready for export." This theme would become the centerpiece of his inaugural and State of the Union addresses in early 2005. In the latter, the president declared that "the best antidote to radicalism and terror is the tolerance and hope kindled in free societies." In the summer of 2005, Secretary of State Condoleezza Rice told a Cairo audience that "things have changed. We had a very rude awakening on September 11th, when I think we realized that our policies to try and promote what we thought was stability in the Middle East had actually allowed, underneath, a very malignant, meaning cancerous, form of extremism to grow up underneath because people didn't have outlets for their political views." The aggressive rhetoric was initially supported by the creation of aid programs with strong democracy components such as the Middle East Partnership Initiative (MEPI).

But with a deteriorating Iraq, an expansionist Iran, and the electoral success of Islamist parties throughout the region, American enthusiasm for promoting democracy began to wane. One Egyptian human rights activist despondently told us in the summer of 2006 that Washington's rhetoric "convinced thousands that the U.S. was serious about democracy and reform. We also believed this, but we were being deceived." Perhaps the most disheartening sign of how far the democratic wave receded in the Middle East came during the 2007 State of the Union address. President Bush singled out "places like Cuba, Belarus, and Burma," for democracy promotion, all safely away from his chaotic, failing experiment in the Arab World.

It is safe to say that the Bush administration's project to promote Middle East democracy failed. It failed because it was

## US Democracy Promotion Must Be Portrayed Realistically

For the United States, it is time to make some decisions regarding the importance we accord to promoting democracy. Georgia will be an important case of America's resolve.

It is important to note here that a U.S. policy of supporting a stronger Georgian state at the expense of democracy is not in [and] of itself a mistake. It is reasonable for U.S. foreign policy to reflect the notion that we are best served by a government in Georgia that is pro-Western, market oriented, supportive of U.S. foreign policy, reasonably popular domestically, but with only a lukewarm commitment to democracy. However, it creates problems when we claim that this government is fully democratic or even fully committed to democracy. As this assertion is increasingly contradicted by the reality in Georgia, it reflects poorly on U.S. foreign policy and the sincerity of our commitment to democracy.... Our failure to criticize Georgia's semi-democracy has made our condemnation of far more repressive systems in the region such as Russia and Kazakhstan sound hollow at times.

*Lincoln A. Mitchell, "Democracy Bound,"*
*National Interest, no. 95, May-June 2008.*

never really tried. With the exception of a brief period in 2004 and 2005 when significant pressure was put on Arab regimes, democracy promotion was little more than a rhetorical device. But lost in the shuffle is the fact that one of the strongest rationales for the "freedom agenda"—that the way to defeat terrorism in the long run is by supporting the growth of democratic institutions—hasn't necessarily been proven wrong, nor should it be so readily discarded due to its unfortunate association with the wrong methods and messengers. But this is precisely what seems to have happened.

## Democracy Is Not a Panacea

In the Fall 2007 *Washington Quarterly*, Francis Fukuyama and Michael McFaul argued that "the loudly proclaimed instrumentalization of democracy promotion in pursuit of U.S. national interests, such as the war on terrorism, taints democracy promotion and makes the United States seem hypocritical when security, economic, or other concerns trump its interests in democracy, as they inevitably will." Around the same time, Thomas Carothers, writing in the *Washington Post*, was more explicit in wishing to disassociate supporting democracy from the fight against terror: "Democracy promotion will need to be repositioned in the war on terrorism, away from the role of rhetorical centerpiece. It's an appealing notion that democratization will undercut the roots of violent Islamic radicalism. Yet democracy is not an antiterrorist elixir. At times democratization empowers political moderates over radicals, but it can also have the opposite effect."

Carothers and others are correct that democracy is not, nor has it ever been, some kind of panacea. To embrace such lofty expectations will only hasten disappointment. Promoting democracy is a difficult business with risks and consequences, among them the chance that emerging or immature democracies might, in the short-term, experience increased political violence and instability. And lack of democracy cannot take the blame for those, like the July 7th London bomber Mohammed Siddique Khan, whose path to terrorism began in [one of] the freest nations in the world. As the histories of some of these jihadists illustrate, powerful cultural and religious forces cannot be ignored.

That said, decoupling support for democracy from the broader effort to combat terrorism and religious extremism in the Middle East would be a costly strategic misstep. If there is indeed a link between lack of democracy and terrorism—and we will argue that there is—then the matter of Middle East democracy is more urgent than it would otherwise be. The question of urgency is not an inconsequential one. Most policymakers and analysts would agree that the region's democratization should, in theory at least, be a long-term goal. But, if it is only considered as such, then it will not figure high on the agenda of an administration with a whole host of other problems, both foreign and domestic, to worry about. However, if the continued dominance of autocratic regimes in the region translates into a greater likelihood of political violence and terrorism, then it becomes an immediate threat to regional stability that the U.S. will need to address sooner rather than later.

## Examining the Tyranny-Terror Link

It is worth emphasizing that democracy promotion does not involve only our relationships with authoritarian allies like Egypt, Jordan, or Saudi Arabia. Our ability and willingness to understand the relationship between autocracy and terror is also intimately tied to future success in Iraq. Drawing on captured documents previously unavailable to the public, a 2008 study by West Point's Combating Terrorism Center found that "low levels of civil liberties are a powerful predictor of the national origin of foreign fighters in Iraq." Of nearly 600 al Qaeda in Iraq fighters listed in the declassified documents, 41 percent were from Saudi Arabia while 19 percent were of Libyan origin. The study also notes that "Saudi Arabian jihadis contribute far more money to [al Qaeda in Iraq] than fighters from other countries." According to the Freedom House index, the Saudi regime is one of the 17 most repressive governments in the world. Because the kingdom brooks no dissent at home, it has, since the early 1980s, sought to bolster its legitimacy by encouraging militants to fight abroad in support of various pan-Islamist causes. Since the late 1990s, those militants have tended to target the United States. In other words, Saudi Arabia's internal politics can have devastating external consequences.

Democratic reform also holds out hope for confronting other Middle Eastern flashpoints. In recent years, the notion of incorporating violent political actors in nonviolent, democratic processes has gained some currency, particularly in light of the successful integration of insurgents in Iraq. Meanwhile, in the Palestinian territories, whatever else one wishes to say about Hamas, the group's electoral participation since 2006 has coincided with a precipitous drop in the suicide bombings that had long been their hallmark.

Recognizing the relevance of democracy to some of the thorniest Middle Eastern conflicts—whose effects reverberate to our shores—makes democracy promotion much harder to dismiss as a luxury of idealism and a purely moral, long-term concern. In short, understanding the interplay between tyranny and terror can allow us to better judge—and, if necessary, elevate— the place of democracy promotion in the hierarchy of national priorities.

## Democracy Promotion Can Improve US Credibility

De-emphasizing support for democracy, on the other hand, will have significant consequences at a time when Arabs and Muslims are looking to us for moral leadership and holding out great expectations for an American president who many continue to see as sympathetic to their concerns. Obama's Cairo speech, hailed throughout the Middle East, was a step in the right direction, but disappointment has since grown as the administration has failed to follow up with tangible policy changes on the ground.

Dropping democracy down on the agenda would ignore the fact that our ideals coincide with those of the majority of Middle Easterners who are angry at us not for promoting democracy, but because we do not. When we say we want democracy but do very little about it, our credibility suffers and we are left open to charges of hypocrisy. This credibility gap should not be dismissed. Ultimately, the fight against terror is not simply about "connecting the dots," improving interagency coordination, and killing terrorists; it is just as important to have a broader vision that addresses the sources of political violence.

Any long-term strategy must take into account an emerging body of evidence which shows that lack of democracy can be a key predictor of terrorism, and correlates with it more strongly than other commonly cited factors like poverty and unemployment. If understood and utilized correctly, democracy promotion can become a key component of a revitalized counterterrorism strategy that tackles the core problem of reducing the appeal of violent extremism in Muslim societies. It has the potential to succeed where the more traditional, hard power components of counterterrorism strategy have failed.

The link between lack of democracy and terrorism also has consequences for American domestic politics. It provides a unifying theme for Democrats and Republicans alike, one that honors our ideals while helping keep us safe and secure. To the extent that politicians have had difficulty selling democracy promotion to the American people, the "tyranny-terror link" provides a promising narrative for U.S. policy in managing the immense challenges of today's Middle East. . . .

## Democracy Promotion Must Take a Multifaceted Approach

A multitude of factors—economic, political, cultural, and religious—contribute to Islamic radicalism and terror. However, one important factor, and one that appears to have a strong empirical basis, is the Middle East's democracy deficit. Any long-term strategy to combat terrorism should therefore include a vigorous, sustained effort to support democracy and democrats in a region long debilitated by autocracy. Obviously, this is an enormous challenge and should not be taken lightly. However, abandoning such a critical task would mean more of the same—a Middle East that continues to fester as a source of political instability and religious extremism. And, in today's world, such instability, and the violence that so often results, cannot be contained; it will spill over and harm America and its allies.

A new democracy promotion strategy in the Middle East should include a variety of measures, including making aid to autocratic regimes conditional on political and human rights reforms; elevating democracy as a crucial part of all high-level bilateral discussions with Arab leaders; coming to terms with the inclusion of nonviolent Islamist parties in the political process; using membership in international organizations as leverage; increasing the budget for programs like the Middle East Partnership Initiative and the Millennium Challenge Account; deepening cooperation with the European Union to spread responsibility; and sponsoring initiatives that bring together Islamist and secular groups to forge inclusive pro-democracy platforms. The pace of democratization should take into account local contexts yet must maintain a consistent focus on expanding the rights of citizens, supporting the development of viable opposition parties, and moving toward free and fair elections.

## The Consensus at Home Must Be for Democracy

But before moving in such a direction, the idea of Middle East democracy must be rehabilitated in the eyes of policymakers and the public alike. Absent a bipartisan political commitment, any new effort will falter. We realize that elevating democracy promotion will mean breaking with the last several decades of U.S. policy, which has relied upon close relationships with Arab regimes at the expense of Arab publics. But our long-term national security, as well as our broader interests in the region, demand such a reorientation. The first step, however, is to reestablish a consensus here at home on both the utility and value of democracy promotion. Once that happens, the discussion of how to actually do it can be conducted with greater clarity. If, on the other hand, we choose to continue along the current path— paying lip service to the importance of democracy abroad but doing increasingly less to actually support it—a great opportunity will be lost.

Turning away from the Arabs and Muslims who overwhelmingly support greater freedom and democracy will rob us of perhaps our strongest weapon in the broader struggle of ideas. For decades, the people of the region have been denied the ability to chart their own course, ask their own questions, and form their own governments. Lack of democratic outlets has pushed people towards extreme methods of opposition and made the resort to terrorist acts more likely. Recognizing this is a crucial step toward a sustained effort to promote Middle East democracy and represents our best chance at a durable and effective counterterrorism policy that protects our vital interests while remaining true to our ideals.

> "The bottom line is that the supposed link between the security of Americans and the spreading of democracy overseas (as well as domestically) is tenuous and remote."

# Promoting Democracy Worldwide Does Not Increase US National Security

*Michael S. Rozeff*

*Democracy promotion overseas has been a main tenet of US national security policy since George W. Bush instituted the Bush Doctrine following the September 11, 2001, terrorist attacks on American soil. In the viewpoint that follows, Michael S. Rozeff makes the case that democracy promotion abroad as a foreign policy tool fails to increase US security. Rozeff presents evidence that throughout history, democracy promotion has failed to improve national security and often has had the opposite effect, earning antagonism from foreign governments and engendering a host of other problems for the country. Rozeff concludes that until this evidence is refuted, the government should abandon this policy. Michael S. Rozeff is a retired finance professor and regular contributor to LewRockwell .com.*

As you read, consider the following questions:

1. As stated by Rozeff, what are the "serious objections" to the strategy of spreading democracy as a tool to increase national security?

2. According to Rozeff, in what types of democracies will economic growth be hampered, and in what types will economic growth be encouraged?

3. What are the "major inherent and severe problems" Rozeff claims accompany a non-neutral foreign policy?

B ush II [George W. Bush] had an explicit national security strategy of spreading democracy throughout the world. The 2006 National Security Strategy goes into this at great length. . . .

Spreading democracy can be done peacefully or via war or via methods that are in between peace and war. Bush believed in unilateral and preventive war as one method.

Now that Bush is gone, is this strategy also gone? It is not. President Obama has the same strategy. He is already applying it. He is only applying it in different ways and with different emphases. . . .

## The Tenuous Link Between Democracy and Security

The notion of making America (and the entire world) secure by ending autocratic governments overseas is the opposite of George Washington's policy of neutrality. It involves making alliances. It involves readiness and willingness to go to war at any time. It involves continual war for the goal of continual peace, virtually a contradiction in terms. It involves some states identifying others as tyrannies and seeking to change their forms of government. It involves the notion that the world can achieve a condition of perpetual peace through the judicious use of armed forces.

Spreading democracy involves the U.S. being policeman of the world. It involves building up and maintaining military forces throughout the world. It involves the U.S. entering wars in which it is not directly a combatant. It involves the U.S. choosing favorites and enemies among other nations. It involves the U.S. in choosing the domestic factions that it supports within foreign nations and making itself the enemy of others.

Under this driving umbrella strategy, the U.S. continually constructs threats where there need not be threats. If it decides to defend Taiwan, then mainland China becomes a threat to the U.S. and an enemy. If it decides that Iraq is in the wrong by invading Kuwait, then it makes war on Iraq. Under this policy, the U.S. for many years supplied arms and support to various dictators and/or autocrats such as Suharto of Indonesia, [Ferdinand] Marcos of the Philippines, Chun Du-Hwan of South Korea, and Saddam Hussein of Iraq.

The strategy is open to abuse. Under this strategy, U.S. foreign policies became shaped by domestic military, financial, agricultural, and other lobbies. States that are entering fights to spread democracy can enter them for reasons of self-interest and advantage to themselves. If two autocratic states like Iraq and Iran are warring, then the U.S. still finds a way to get involved.

The strategy faces operational problems. Who is to identify the instances when states violate rights? Who is to be the judge and jury of the suspected rights violations, the disputes, and the conflicts arising among states? What happens when two or more states both think they are in the right? Is any use of armed force by any state to be taken as evidence that it is in the wrong? Which disputes will be the occasion for American force to be used, and which will not?

Even more serious objections to the strategy are these:

- democracy itself is not an ideal form of government
- governments can have democratic forms and still be tyrannies

- governments can have non-democratic forms and still be peaceful
- democracies are not necessarily any more peaceful than other forms of government
- democracies can inhibit other goals like economic well-being and progress
- other forms of government can be consistent with economic progress
- self-determination of peoples does not necessarily lead them to choose democracy

The bottom line is that the supposed link between the security of Americans and spreading democracy overseas (as well as domestically) is tenuous and remote. It does not really exist, as will be argued further below.

## The Bush Doctrine Is Flawed

Bush was obliged by law to publish annually a National Security Strategy [NSS] document, under the Goldwater-Nichols Act. It is supposed to be the outcome of a serious effort by our top officials to plan strategy and make it public. Bush did this in 2002 and 2006, but not in 2003, 2004, 2005, and 2007.

Obama hasn't yet come out with the 2008 document, even though he has already announced his Afghanistan strategy. . . .

Nicholas J. Armstrong of the Institute for National Security and Counterterrorism has come out with an article that is highly critical of the strategy of spreading democracy *as Bush operated it*. . . . He says

> . . . the Bush administration's recent strategy documents possess significant shortcomings that led to important policy failures. A problematic rationale for the preemptive use of force, weak justifications and inconsistencies in democracy promotion, and a lack of strategic priorities are just a few criticisms among others.

## Democracy Promotion Creates Disposable People

American democracy, as we have seen it, has not brought any kind of positive change in the democracy converts like Iraq and Afghanistan. On occasions, it is used as a precondition for economic growth or used synonymously with corporate globalization and free trade. In practice, it is anything but democratic. Decisions taken at IMF [International Monetary Fund] and WB [World Bank] never take place with the consent of poor countries. The undemocratic forces of liberal democracy create an idea of a disposable people, create alienation among them and push them to religious fundamentalism. Though called liberal democracy, free market creates everything opposed to democracy: unilateralism, terrorism and hegemony.

*Jyotirmaya Tripathy, "Democracy and Its Others,"* Journal of Third World Studies, *vol. 27, no. 1, Spring 2010.*

In other words, the Bush team didn't think through their methods and operated haphazardly.

The current strategic assessment of the external security environment suffers from two significant weaknesses: the unrealistic notion that democracy promotion must underpin the actions of the U.S. abroad, and the flawed presumption that democracy promotion is the solution to transnational terrorism. Undoubtedly, terrorism is a significant threat to U.S. national security, but the most recent NSS illogically assumes that terrorism demands global democratization.

This is a much broader criticism. It says two things. Spreading democracy is not a realistic foundation or center point for foreign policy; and the nation should not address terrorism by spreading democracy. He goes on:

> . . . the *preemptive* use of force—supported by an entangled justification of eliminating *future* threats while promoting democracy—creates an imbalance in retributive justice and thereby undermines the moral legitimacy of all U.S. democracy promotion efforts abroad, regardless of intent.

This says that the Bush Doctrine is morally flawed and its application works against the U.S. . . .

## Democracy Does Not Necessarily Improve Security

Before turning to the empirical side, let us think through some theory to analyze the question.

Why do people want security anyway? Security is desirable so that people may enhance their welfare. If free markets and property rights are suppressed by means of government measures enacted in democracies, then security is reduced and, by the same token, welfare may be reduced for many millions of persons that comprise substantial minorities or even for most of the entire society.

A relevant question is then whether or not democracy has a positive effect on economic growth. If it does not, then it means that democracy does not really enhance welfare. If democracy enhanced security, it should have a positive effect on economic growth and welfare. If democracy fails to enhance even domestic welfare, then the notion that spreading democracy to foreign lands will enhance domestic security and thus allow higher domestic welfare has to be seen as very far-fetched and very unlikely. In fact, if democracy lowers welfare, and there is evidence that it does, then by actively making foreign countries poorer, the U.S. is encouraging foreign people to rise up and resist America.

In those democracies in which government's limits are expansible, voting occurs on more and more goods, such as health care, education, and energy use, that once belonged to private decision-making. Under these conditions, democracy brings increasing violation of rights and increasing democratic totalitarianism. It brings the increasing influence of lobbies for interest groups. This powerful process hampers economic growth. It is not easily reversed. Under these conditions, we will observe that political democracy and economic growth are negatively related.

On the other hand, in democracies that are replacing rapacious autocracies that have constricted the property rights and the economy, we may observe small and weak states and high economic growth if the democracy is associated with these conditions that free up the economy.

The key variables in economic growth *are not democracy per se*. They are such things as personal responsibility, respect for private property rights, private solutions to private problems, not collectivizing the economy and creating commons problems, low taxes, low barriers to entry, small government, and low regulation. If a state is weak and democratic, it may be conducive to economic growth. If it is strong and democratic, it may suppress growth.

A society does need security so that investment will be encouraged, including investment in human capital, but democracy is not a form of government that necessarily increases security.

So much for theory. What's the evidence? In 1983, Erich Weede (in the journal *Kyklos*) examined the impact of democracy on economic growth. The time period studied was 1960–79. He examined data for 124 countries. He found:

> There is a clearly significant (at the 2% level) negative effect of political democracy on economic growth, however measured.

Weede went on to look at those countries in which "government revenue as a percentage of GDP exceeds 20%." His findings are remarkable:

For these nations, many of the control variables lose most of their importance, in particular for GDP growth rates. Truly staggering, however, are the results in the democracy row of *Table 4*. Here it is obvious that political democracy is a major barrier to economic growth in those countries where the state strongly interferes in the economy.

While democracy is not harmful in weak states or states that are small relative to the economy, it is clearly harmful in strong states or states that are large relative to the economy. (This includes the U.S.) Where democracy entails collectivization, it slows down economic growth. Where government is large, there is pooling of resources and control of them by government. . . . Economic growth slows. . . .

## The Problems of Non-Neutrality

Those who, like Paul Wolfowitz [U.S. Deputy Secretary of Defense under George W. Bush], think that spreading democracy overseas enhances American security and welfare should come forward and present their *theory and evidence* that it does.

Where is there evidence that America is even capable of accomplishing this goal, much less that the goal makes any sense? The American occupation of Haiti from 1915 to 1934 certainly did not help Haiti or the average American. American imperialism seems often enough to be the American goal.

The rhetoric of our leaders is not enough. They have had their way for 100 years, the latest instance being in Iraq. Not only is the theory of spreading democracy to promote American security subject to many severe criticisms to the point that it makes no sense, but in practice it runs afoul of many difficulties. Iraq provides a good illustration of this. Vietnam provides another.

A foreign policy of non-neutrality has several truly major inherent and severe problems:

- inability to recognize politically dynamic forces as they are occurring
- inability to forecast the path of politically dynamic forces
- catalyzing new political forces by interfering in another nation
- being held hostage to events initiated by political forces in another nation
- having policy captured by domestic and foreign interest groups
- being drawn into the fights of others
- having to deal with the actions and reactions of neighbors who have interests in the country being interfered with

The leaders of a nation that is intent on interfering with other nations and supporting movements that it deems anti-autocratic face all these problems and more. . . .

## The Continuation of a Flawed Policy

Are Obama's strategic positions any better on Afghanistan and Pakistan than Bush's on Iraq? Are they any less intent on spreading democracy? Not at all.

The White House calls for "realistic and achievable objectives." Their first objective is not unreasonable as these things go. It is to disrupt the terrorists in the region and stop them from conducting terrorist attacks. The next objective is Wilsonian. It is:

> Promoting a more capable, accountable, and effective government in Afghanistan that serves the Afghan people and can eventually function, especially regarding internal security, with limited international support.

It is one thing to go after terrorists, as Jefferson went after pirates, although going after them on land has certain difficulties of territory and sovereignty that need to be ironed out. But putting those things aside, it is entirely another matter to get involved with building a government for Afghanistan. That continues the same old policy of spreading democracy that has no sound basis. It's the Bush policy all over again. Mixing that up with hunting down terrorists is strategic confusion. It is in fact quite amazing to read the White House's explicit intention to bolster the legitimacy of the Afghan government!

Obama is also aiming to strengthen "Afghan security forces." These forces do not necessarily represent the interests of various warlords in Afghanistan, which means that Obama aims to interfere in this way again in Afghanistan politics.

That is not all. Obama also aims at:

> Assisting efforts to enhance civilian control and stable constitutional government in Pakistan and a vibrant economy that provides opportunity for the people of Pakistan.

This spells involvement in the domestic politics of a second large and turbulent country. Neighboring countries like Iran, India, and China have interests in Pakistan and Afghanistan. This means involvement with the reactions of these nations.

## US Foreign Policy Repeats Itself

The American empire has had a consistent policy for 100 years: national security via spreading democracy. Obama is adhering to this policy. However, overseas democracy is neither necessary nor sufficient for security in America.

Theory suggests that democracy has a negative relation to economic welfare, especially as states get larger and infringe more greatly on property rights. Empirical studies over a hundred countries and several decades do not support the hypothesis that democracy enhances economic growth. If anything, they support a negative relation. To the extent that economic growth is a form of security and enhances security, domestic democracy reduces security.

If a foreign democracy has reduced economic growth, why would that enhance U.S. security? There is no good reason. One might expect that less prosperous nations might have a greater tendency and incentive to become trouble spots.

When the U.S. actually goes about the practical business of enhancing democracy in foreign lands, it runs into a host of problems that necessarily arise from the nature of interfering in the politics of others. The costs are high, often very high and long continued. They fall on the average American. Any benefits are showered upon specific interest groups, like Lockheed Martin, farmers, consultants, and Halliburton. It may also have appeal to those who mistakenly think they are doing God's work through the State.

If there is no known general benefit to the average American from this strategy and high costs, the strategy of promoting national security through spreading democracy appears to be irrational from their point of view.

It is my guess that Obama has not thought through the meaning of the strategy any more than he has thought through his Keynesianism. I think that our elected government officials do some thinking and questioning and shaping of positions so that they can get elected, but that, by and large, they unthinkingly accept the main assumptions of American strategies. They tinker around the edges but they do not really alter anything. Even when their rhetoric suggests something more radical, their actions retreat to the status quo. A Kennedy will send more advisers to South Vietnam and attempt to control its government. Domestically, they go about their usual business of making the democracy more and more totalitarian. Occasionally a Nixon will go to China, but it won't matter much because at home he and the American leadership will ignore the kinds of policies that might liberalize the economy and instead promote those that destabilize it and slow it down. And in foreign policy, they will stick to the same old Wilsonianism that should be thoroughly discredited and that has not served America well.

> *"America should now practice what it preaches and support real democratic movements in the region, even if we do not always like their policies."*

# The United States Should Promote True Democracy in the Middle East

*Eric Margolis*

*The history of American involvement in Middle Eastern politics has emphasized so-called stability and moderation over true democracy, argues Eric Margolis in the following viewpoint. This policy, he states, has led to collusion with dictators, turning a blind eye to brutal methods of enforcing the status quo, and ensuring that American interests remained protected. Margolis therefore sees the 2011 democratic protests in the region to be as much about reacting against US influence in the region as revolting against the autocratic leaders of the individual countries. To respond to this discontent, the author believes that the United States should drop the façade of democratic promotion it has hidden behind for decades and openly assist the people throughout the Middle East to establish true democratic governments. Eric Margolis is a journalist and author of* War at the Top of the World *and* American Raj: Domination or Liberation.

As you read, consider the following questions:

1. As stated by the author, what does "moderation" in the Middle East entail and how was it encouraged by the United States?
2. What two examples of free elections does Margolis give and what were their outcomes?
3. To what historical example does the author compare the current situation in Egypt?

The Mideast house of cards so laboriously constructed by Washington over the past four decades threatens to collapse. One can't help but be reminded of the revolts across Eastern Europe in 1989 that began the fall of the Soviet Empire.

Now it may be the turn of America's Mideast empire, an empire constructed of Arab dictatorships to assure U.S. domination of oil and Israel's domination of the Levant. The popular uprisings against Western-backed dictatorships that erupted in Tunisia, spread to Egypt, and have been flaring in Yemen, Jordan, and Morocco, are the result of Washington's dedication to what it calls "stability" and "moderation."

Yet we should note that the current uprising against Western-sponsored military rule in the Mideast did not begin in Tunisia, but with a slow-motion, barely noticed process in Turkey, where the moderate democratic AK party of Prime Minister Recep Erdogan has driven the Turkish army back to its barracks and out of politics. Turkey's ousting of its mighty military, which had ruled the nation behind a flimsy façade of parliamentary puppets since the 1940s, electrified the Muslim world. Turkey broke its close links to Israel and championed the cause of Palestine.

Egypt's military dictator, General-President Hosni Mubarak, who ruled with an iron fist since 1981, was fulsomely hailed in the West for the twin qualities of stability and moderation. His unloving people may have called him "pharaoh," but to successive administrations in Washington, he was a "valued, democratic statesman." The rulers of Morocco, Algeria, Tunisia, Jordan and Yemen—not to mention the oil monarchs of the Arabian Peninsula—were also lauded as moderates, guardians of stability, even democrats.

## The American Policy of Stability

Stability, in the American lexicon, means not allowing any opposition parties or individuals to trouble the status quo, be they political Islamists or secular democrats. Challenging the Mideast's Pax Americana became a subversive act that was usually branded terrorism and linked to the shadowy Osama bin Laden and his almost non-existent movement, al-Qaeda. The mere mention by Mideast autocrats of the dreaded Q-word was sufficient to hush American concerns about egregious violations of human rights by their satraps or the crushing of all opposition. The al-Qaeda bogeyman was certain to produce hefty infusions of U.S. military aid.

I chose the title of my latest book about how the U.S. rules the Arab world *American Raj* to underline the remarkable similarity between the control methods used by imperial Britain in India and those employed by its successor empire, the United States. "Raj" means imperium through local rulers. And that's just the structure built by the U.S. across the Mideast.

"Stability" has been enforced by brutal secret police using torture and extra-judicial executions. In Egypt, a favorite punishment for male protesters and candidates who dared run in rigged elections against Mubarak was anal rape. Across the region, behind the secret police stood U.S. and French-equipped Arab armies whose primary military mission was to suppress their own people and prevent revolution. Battalions of informers, and dismissal from government jobs or housing and pension plans, were all common tools used to dissuade anti-regime activities. Press censorship was universal.

Such was the "stability" cultivated and financed by the U.S. and, in North Africa, by France. "Moderation," in turn, means being obedient to Washington's demands, acting against all reformers and revolutionaries, and making nice to Israel. Egypt was paid $2 billion per annum—it was the second highest recipient of foreign aid after Israel—to abandon the Palestinian cause. Tens of millions of "black" payments went to Egyptian generals, politicians, officials, and media.

## The Possibility of Free Elections Remains Elusive

But the foundations of the Raj are now gravely threatened by the spontaneous popular uprisings in the long-suffering Arab world. Ironically, the Mideast is finally getting a potent dose of the democracy that neoconservatives used to claim they were promoting. In their vocabulary, democracy really meant obedient regimes that were quietly friendly to Israel and never allowed unruly elements to surface.

Such ersatz democracies always meant rigged elections. America willingly closed its eyes to—or even abetted—these fraudulent votes across the Mideast, including in U.S.-occupied Iraq and in Afghanistan. After the Soviets invaded Afghanistan, they actually used to run somewhat more "honest" rigged elections than the Americans who followed them into Kabul years later.

In fact, there have been only two free elections in the Arab world. The first, in 1991 in Algeria, resulted in a landslide for moderate Islamists. Paris and Washington quickly backed the Algerian army in crushing the vote and jailing its victors.

The second free election occurred in Palestine in 2006. Hamas decisively defeated the Palestinian Authority government of Mahmoud Abbas, which was funded and guided by the U.S. and Israel, as confirmed by recent document leaks. The U.S., failing to overthrow Hamas, locked it up in the Gaza open-air prison in collaboration with Mubarak's Egypt.

It was clear that free votes across the Arab world (and in Pakistan) would unseat most U.S.-backed regimes and produce either rambunctious democracies or government by various forms of Islamists, ranging from the cautious moderates of the Egyptian Brotherhood and Turkey's AK party to Sunni fire-brands. That could bring higher oil prices and problems for Israel.

Most important, collapse of the Raj threatens to destroy one of the pillars of U.S. world power: *control* of oil. America does not need to import Mideast oil, but it is determined to continue controlling the Arab states that produce oil, which gives Washington huge leverage over Europe, India, China, and Japan.

## The "Cauldron of Anger and Discontent"

The explosions that began in January in the Mideast confirmed that the entire region is a cauldron of anger and discontent. Little Tunisia, with only 10.8 million people, ignited the conflagration when the thievery and arrogance of its dictator of three decades, General Ben Ali, became too much to bear for even the easy-going Tunisians. Interestingly, Ben Ali had heeded Washington's half-hearted calls for more democracy—of the U.S.-approved kind—by winning his last rigged election only by a cliff-hanging 89 percent rather than his usual 95 percent or even 98 percent.

Neoconservatives and their supporters, as well as many in the foreign-policy establishment, are now trying to deflect attention from the embarrassing failure of their Mideast policies by claiming the twin causes of the uprisings were demographics and Islamic fundamentalism.

Demography indeed played an important role in Mideast unrest. Twelve years ago I warned about the "onrushing tidal wave of young people that would swamp all Mideast governments" and pointed out there were not enough schools, apartments, jobs, or even food and water for the coming human inundation.

Half the Arab world's people are under 30, and of course high unemployment in the stagnant economics of the Mideast is an explosive issue. So is pervasive corruption at all levels that was

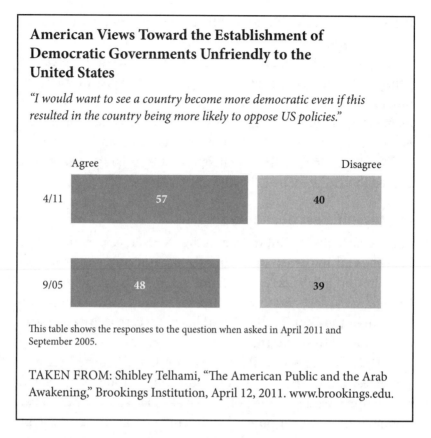

**American Views Toward the Establishment of Democratic Governments Unfriendly to the United States**

*"I would want to see a country become more democratic even if this resulted in the country being more likely to oppose US policies."*

| | Agree | Disagree |
|---|---|---|
| 4/11 | 57 | 40 |
| 9/05 | 48 | 39 |

This table shows the responses to the question when asked in April 2011 and September 2005.

TAKEN FROM: Shibley Telhami, "The American Public and the Arab Awakening," Brookings Institution, April 12, 2011. www.brookings.edu.

often encouraged by the U.S. doling out money to key groups in the establishment. Discontent has been stoked by the total lack of real justice in the Arab world or Pakistan—this is a principal reason for the popularity of Islamic parties and swift, effective, but often draconian Sharia law.

But the most important detonator of recent events was fury at being compelled to follow policies hated by the peoples of the Mideast. Arabs from Morocco to Iraq have been enraged and shamed by seeing their governments adopt friendly or at least non-confrontational policies toward Israel and abandoning or even oppressing the Palestinians, whose suffering is the prime force producing anti-Western anger in the Muslim world. Thanks to al-Jazeera TV and the Internet, the plight of the

Palestinians is now viewed nightly by tens of millions across the Muslim world.

In particular, Mubarak's collusion with Israel and the U.S. in jailing Palestinians in Gaza and trying to starve them into submission infuriated Egyptians. He was widely branded a traitor to his people and to the Palestinians and an arch-collaborator with Israel. It was no coincidence that Mubarak holed up at Sharm el-Sheikh in Sinai, a short helicopter ride to Israel. Unlike the United States, Israel usually sticks by its friends and allies.

## Replays of Past Scenarios

The scenario played out in Iran in the 1970s. Its ruler, Shah Reza Pahlavi, and the grasping entourage of courtiers and businessmen around him sneered at Islamic religion and culture, put on Western airs, and readily accepted the role as Washington's policeman of the Gulf. Mubarak and his predecessor, Anwar Sadat, also followed this pattern.

The Shah supported Israel, sold it oil, and scorned pleas of the Palestinians for help. Israel and the U.S. trained the Shah's notoriously brutal secret police, Savak, just as they have been doing with the secret police and intelligence agencies of Egypt, Morocco, and Jordan which are virtually branches of CIA, just as Eastern Europe's little KGBs were subsidiaries of Moscow Center.

In Iran, Washington put all its political eggs in one basket. When the Shah was overthrown by a popular uprising, decades of U.S. policy went down the drain. America's support of the Shah and his secret police, and CIA's overthrow of the democratic [Mohammad] Mossadegh government, turned Iranians violently against the United States and engendered decades of hatred and poisoned relations between two nations that should be friends and natural allies.

Now the same process is occurring in Egypt and throughout the American Raj. Mideast regimes have kept bending over to placate American policy demands until one day, like plastic, they snap without warning. What's left after the inevitable explosions is seething anti-American bitterness.

## Hypocrisy in Middle East Policy

Ignore all the platitudes over Egypt coming from official Washington. While calling for democracy in the Arab world, the U.S. has been the godfather of dictatorship and repression for the past five decades. It takes a strong stomach to watch members of the Obama administration like Hillary Clinton or Vice President Biden, who used to call Mubarak a "democrat" and laud his "moderate" leadership, suddenly begin ask for an "orderly transition to democracy."

Hypocrisy is by no means exclusive to Washington: after revolts erupted in Tunisia, France's newly-appointed bumbling foreign minister actually offered Tunis tough French riot police to put down pro-democracy demonstrations. Britain, France, Canada, and Italy all backed Mideast dictatorships without the slightest compunctions.

Israel and its neoconservative partisans are now in high gear warning that it's either the Mubarak police state—with or without him—or firebrand, Iranian-style mullahs. These neocon alarms are no more credible than their self-serving falsehoods about the supposed dangers of Saddam Hussein. Easy-going Sunni Egypt is nothing like Shia Iran. So far, politicized religion has played almost no role in the great Egyptian revolt. But if legitimate demands by Egyptians for democracy and an end to four decades of police-state repression are not met, the revolution may well turn extreme.

Mubarak said on Feb. 1 [2011] that he would not "run" for president in Egypt's next rigged election this fall. His day has clearly passed. But the U.S. national-security establishment and supporters of Israel are hoping that the iron-fisted police apparatus that kept Mubarak in power for three decades, and Sadat before that, will still keep its grip on Egypt behind some sort of pliant new leader. The U.S. has groomed the hated intelligence chief Omar

Suleiman to replace the 82-year-old Mubarak. It is also likely the CIA has designated backup generals to be Egypt's next ruler if Suleiman stumbles.

## The Time to Enact Democratic Change Has Come

But Egyptians want real freedom. The last Egyptian leader who was not a tool of Western interests was the widely beloved Gamal Abdel Nasser, who died or was assassinated in 1970. Nasser was Egypt's first truly Egyptian ruler since the days of the ancient pharaohs.

How else might the endgame play out? Younger officers in Egypt's 450,000-man armed forces could stage a coup—just as Nasser's Young Officers did—putting the country on a nationalist course and restoring Egypt as the military, political, economic, and cultural center of the Arab world. Under Mubarak, Egypt has been a colonial backwater.

But Egypt's independence is constrained by poverty and lack of land. The nation, whose arable land is only the size of Maryland, cannot feed its 84–85 million people and has become the world's largest wheat importer through a major U.S. food-aid program, authorized by Congress—a program that has been rife with egregious illegalities and kickbacks.

The new Arab Intifada presents the United States with a golden opportunity to junk five decades of counter-productive, contradictory Mideast policy that has led to 9/11 and anti-American hatred across the Muslim world. America should now practice what it preaches and support real democratic movements in the region, even if we do not always like their policies. Americans must stop turning Islam into a bogeyman employed to thwart a viable Palestinian peace and sustain Israel's expansionist ambitions.

Creating a viable Palestinian state lies at the heart of this transformative process. Our old imperial policies and neo-conservative fantasies have failed. Fostering real peace in the Mideast would do all its people, including Israelis and Palestinians, an historic service. This is what the America of Jefferson, Madison, and Eisenhower would have done. Arabs have been waiting for 50 years for America to show them the way to real democracy, social justice, and economic growth. The moment has arrived.

> *"The United States must pay attention to its interests—which coincide with its values."*

# Promoting Democracy in the Middle East Should Benefit US Interests

*Mortimer B. Zuckerman*

*In the wake of the 2011 uprisings across the Middle East, many commentators expressed hope about the transition to democracy in the region. However others have remained skeptical about the prospect for the establishment of genuine democracies. In the following viewpoint, Mortimer B. Zuckerman warns that in supporting democratic change, the United States must always be mindful of the outcomes of this transition and encourage change that coincides with American interests and values. Zuckerman worries that the current transition could install leaders who would be detrimental to US involvement in the Middle East. He offers the Muslim Brotherhood's belief in Islamic law as one example of the potentially negative views that could become prominent in Egyptian politics. Mortimer B. Zuckerman is the editor-in-chief of* U.S. News & World Report.

As you read, consider the following questions:

1. As stated by Zuckerman, what are some of the beliefs of the Muslim Brotherhood?
2. What are some of the examples given by the author of the consequences if the United States allows the influence of Islamic, anti-American parties to become strong forces in the Middle East?
3. According to the author, what is the "most reliable institution in Egypt"?

The political revolution in Egypt and its spread to other parts of the Islamic sphere have riveted the world and its media. Where is all of this headed? Nobody really knows. Not the commentators, not the intelligence community, not in the West, not in the East, not the Egyptians, and not the media.

This is no small issue, for Egypt has often set the political tone for the whole of the Middle East. Today Baghdad is in chaos. Amman and the king of Jordan, the Palestine Liberation Organization [PLO], and Bahrain are all swaying in the wind. Beirut has already fallen to [Shi'a Muslim militants and political party] Hezbollah extremists. Gaza has fallen to [Palestinian Islamist party] Hamas. We are living on the fault line of an earthquake.

## The Possibility of an Islamic Democracy

The Obama administration and the media talk about Egypt as if it is on the verge of democracy, but former British Prime Minister Tony Blair put his finger on the fallacy: "You don't just have a government and a movement for democracy. You also have others, notably the Muslim Brotherhood, who would take this in a different direction." His concern is that democracy in Egypt may well be an interim phase en route to a new dictatorship predicated on extremist Islam. Democracy is not achieved by opening voting booths. A responsible democracy requires laws and their enforcement to ensure that the voting is incorruptible and the results are representative. There has to be an independent judiciary, the rule of law, an open, plural, and independent press, and a culture of human rights. For all the euphoria of a spontaneous uprising, it cannot just be assumed that Egypt now has these elements or a political culture that can sustain a liberal democratic regime. Only a few revolutions develop as well as the one that began in Boston in 1775; others (Paris 1789, Moscow 1917, Teheran 1979) were, shall we say, a disappointment.

Nobody knows the true strength of the Muslim Brotherhood among the young or in Egyptian society as a whole. Nobody knows what the composition of the next Egyptian parliament might be, once it is elected in free, rather than fraudulent, elections. What we do know is that the Muslim Brotherhood is the only organized force within the opposition and as such has the best chance to exploit the post-revolutionary confusion. In the aftermath of a revolution, the people who seize power need not be the most popular, only the most organized, and in Egypt that is the Muslim Brotherhood. It believes in what? It believes in an Islamic democracy based on the principles of sharia, or Islamic law, and the investiture of a supreme guide—something eerily similar to Iran's Islamic state. Islam has a unique appeal in Egypt and indeed in the broader Arab world where secular dictators ruled for decades except in the mosques, which they were unable to close. So the mosques became the center of political activism and Islam the doctrine of opposition.

## Egyptians Favor an Islamic State and Sharia

The Brotherhood opposes a secular state as well as Western civilization, but supports *taqiyya*, which means lying is allowed if it helps to ultimately defeat the infidels. As for the Brotherhood mellowing, a notion that is the love child of our mass media, this mostly reflects the organization's recruitment of media-savvy spokesmen, who can espouse the virtues of a pro-democracy platform as a smokescreen for the group's real views and intentions.

Polls in Egypt reveal that the people want democracy—but that they also want an Islamic state with sharia and all of its restraints on minorities, religion, and women. As Robert Satloff of the Washington Institute for Near East Policy said this month, "The Muslim Brotherhood is not, as some suggest, simply an Egyptian version of the March of Dimes." Opinion polls of Egyptians in past years indicate that 60 percent or more support Islamists and favor the re-establishment of a single Islamic state, or caliphate. In a Pew poll last spring, fully three quarters of Egyptians said they favored strict sharia punishments, and of those who saw a struggle between fundamentalists and groups that want to modernize the country, only 27 percent favored modernizers. Half expressed favorable views of Hamas, 30 percent Hezbollah, and 20 percent al-Qaeda. If these convictions or inclinations govern Egypt's future politics, ousted President Hosni Mubarak's military authoritarianism might well be replaced by Islamic authoritarianism.

Remember when Egyptians had the chance to choose their legislators in 2005? Where they could, they favored the totalitarian Muslim Brotherhood. If that happens again, the United States' greatest ally in the region will become its greatest enemy, and Israel's peace partner will become its greatest foe. As Bernard Lewis, the renowned historian of Islam, said recently: "Many of our so-called friends in the region are inefficient kleptocracies. But they're better than the Islamic radicals." It's a judgment that is well captured in the phrase "the evil of two lessers."

## The US Should Remain Cautious in Supporting Democratic Change

We should not do anything that would strengthen Islamic, pro-Iranian, anti-American political parties. That is what happened in Iran, where the Islamists took over with their powerful and disciplined forces, killing or exiling secular pro-democratic politicians; in the Gaza Strip, where premature legislative elections gave a victory to Hamas; and in Lebanon, where the government is now dominated by Hezbollah. All these parties pledged nonviolence, only to reveal that those who murder can surely lie. The leader or supreme guide of the Muslim Brotherhood in Egypt, Mohammed Badie, made no bones about it in a sermon last year: "The history of freedom is not written in ink but in blood." Exploiting the democratic process to establish an Islamic regime is the Brotherhood's entryway to power.

Think of what would happen if Iran poured millions and millions of dollars into the Muslim Brotherhood so it could disburse the money to the vast proportions of the Egyptian population who live on less than $2 a day in order to influence the election. Then we may recall the words of the great Irish poet W.B. Yeats: "The blood-dimmed tide is loosed and everywhere the ceremony of innocence is drowned."

How would America handle such a catastrophe? How would it react to a leadership committed to the decapitation or stoning of gays, adulterers, and apostates; that endorses amputating the limbs of petty thieves; and that sanctifies suicide bombings and promotes genocide? Remember what happened in Gaza in 2006 when there was a reckless rush to elections without a foundation of democratic institutions. Once Hamas was in power, its version of democracy included throwing political rivals off rooftops, shooting opponents in the kneecaps, and executing women. The Hamas-dominated Palestinian parliament has not convened in the three years since that violence, and Hamas leaders say the party will boycott elections that the Palestinian Authority has called for.

## Democracy in Egypt Must Be Stable and Authentic

Secretary of State Hillary Clinton has wisely resisted playing to the gallery on Egypt. "It needs to be an orderly, peaceful transition to real democracy," she said early this month. "Not faux democracy." This is the heart of the matter. America cannot sanctify an election process and ignore the risks of the outcome.

Egyptian society needs time to prepare for elections and to remediate the effects of years of government oppression. Non-Islamist parties must have an opportunity to emerge and fill in the intervening political space to compete with the Brotherhood. We must give secular democrats a chance, for if Egypt's revolution is usurped by the Brotherhood, the emergence of an autocratic strongman, far worse than Mubarak, will only be a matter of time. The test is not the first election, but rather whether there can be a second fair election.

The most reliable institution in Egypt is the army. It is the anchor of stability, continuity, and, ironically enough, peace as well. Its popular image is "defender of the homeland," and its veterans are perceived as war heroes. Properly inspired, the Egyptian army can provide a bridge to a future civilian government in Cairo. It can play a vital role in modernizing Egyptian society and checking the excesses of religious politics. It can introduce a new constitution that enjoys broad support and includes checks and balances that would make it difficult for minorities to rule majorities.

## US Interests Play a Role in Middle East Change

President Obama might well recall what he wrote in *Foreign Affairs* in the summer of 2007: "In the Islamic world and beyond, combating the terrorists' prophets of fear will require more than lectures on democracy." The United States must pay attention to its interests—which coincide with its values. A Brotherhood government would assault individual liberty and would be a disaster for the United States. It would be able to deploy one of the strongest militaries in the region, built on some of the most advanced American-made platforms. It would support terrorism efforts worldwide and combat antiterrorism efforts. It would strengthen Hamas and undermine the PLO. It would put Jordan's King Abdullah under even more pressure. It would threaten Israel in the short run, and in the long run might expose Israel to another "1948 moment" in the form of a multi-front war, with overwhelming odds.

America needs to be on the right side of human rights. It also needs to be on the right side of history. Our interests and our values are at stake in the outcome of the revolution taking place in Egypt, where our policies should reflect the advice: "Do not take the slightest risk of a catastrophic outcome."

> *"The failure to bring democracies together will not mean sustaining an acceptable status quo; it will mean continued inadequate and ineffective responses to the many problems that now transcend international borders."*

# A League of Democracies Would Benefit the World and Advance Democracy

*James M. Lindsay*

*James M. Lindsay argues in the following viewpoint that the creation of a "league of democracies"—also called a "concert of democracies"—would benefit not only those countries that joined the coalition but also the rest of the world as well. He outlines the criteria for membership, advocating standards such as proof of regular democratic elections, upholding of individual rights, and governing by rule of law. Countries not in accordance with these guidelines could strive to achieve them and then gain the benefits of membership such as open trade. Lindsay concludes that the establishment of this type of league poses the best chance for the most powerful countries in the world to solve the most pressing global*

James M. Lindsay, "The Case for a Concert of Democracies," *Ethics & International Affairs*, vol. 23, no. 1, 2009. Copyright © 2009 Carnegie Council for Ethics in International Affairs. Reprinted with the permission of Cambridge University Press.

*problems. James M. Lindsay is the senior vice president, director of studies, and Maurice R. Greenberg Chair at the Council on Foreign Relations.*

As you read, consider the following questions:

1. What does Lindsay believe would be the three main tasks of the proposed concert of democracies?
2. As stated by Lindsay, what two premises would the success of the concert depend upon?
3. What evidence does Lindsay give to support his claim that the concert would not trigger a new Cold War?

Globalization has remade the world we once knew. We now live in an era in which dangerous developments anywhere can have devastating consequences everywhere. Terrorism is an obvious example: a few young men born in Riyadh and trained in the Hindu Kush can turn jetliners into weapons of mass destruction in New York and Washington. Infectious disease is another: a person with a particularly virulent form of flu could board a plane in Hong Kong and inadvertently spread sickness to every corner of the globe. Or international finance: the collapse of the housing market in Northern California can trigger a major financial panic and push us to the brink of a global depression.

A world in which problems cross borders so easily is one in which broad-based multilateral cooperation is essential. Today, however, we lack international institutions that are capable of prompt and effective action. Over a whole range of challenges, the world is essentially undergoverned. The institutions we do have were created in a different time for different purposes. They all too often reflect the geopolitical realities of a world that no longer exists, and are incapable of meeting the challenges we now face.

New institutions are now needed that recognize how much the world has changed and that mobilize those states most capable of meeting the dangers we confront. One such institution would bring together the world's established democracies into a single organization dedicated to joint action—what has been called a "League" or "Concert" of Democracies. The world's democracies are powerful and capable. Most important, they share an essential value in a globalizing world—a common dedication to ensuring the life, liberty, and happiness of free peoples.

## Mandate and Membership

A Concert of Democracies would have three primary tasks: to help democracies confront their mutual security challenges, to promote economic growth and development among its members as well as globally, and to promote the expansion of democracy and human rights. The concert would achieve these ends by providing a vehicle through which its members could share information, coordinate strategies, harmonize policies, and take action together. The concert would not just act on its own: its members would work through other international institutions, including the United Nations, to mobilize democracies and autocracies alike to meet pressing global challenges.

Who should be able to join the Concert of Democracies? One criterion for membership must be regular, free, and fair elections. But that is just a start. Concert members should also guarantee the rights of individuals within their countries. Their citizens must enjoy both fundamental political rights (to vote, organize, and participate in government) and basic civil rights (to speak, assemble, and freely practice their religion), and those rights must be guaranteed by the rule of law. Moreover, the commitment to uphold individual rights and govern by the rule of law should be so rooted in their societies that the chances of a reversion to autocratic rule are for practical purposes unthinkable. (The Community of Democracies launched in Warsaw in 2000 has far more relaxed admission criteria, which is why its membership has included such countries as Afghanistan, Bahrain, and Jordan.)

Roughly sixty countries meet the membership criteria of regular competitive elections, protection of individual rights,

## On Membership in International Organizations

The United Nations, at least as regards certain objectives it was intended to attain, has included constituencies in its membership, which, at best, will not support those objectives, and at worst, will work to impede their attainment.

The membership of an international organization determines its potentials and limits. An organization whose founding treaty assigns it the task of regulating salmon stocks in the North Pacific would do well to include Russia, Japan, Canada, and the United States. To include Switzerland, Paraguay, and Chad would be, at best, superfluous. If such countries actively participated in such an organization, they well could impede its main work, even if their intentions were entirely benign. . . . Non-fishing members well may have no malign intent; they nevertheless may undermine the purposes of an organization. In the real world of general international organizations, like the United Nations, it cannot be assumed that all participants are benignly motivated. Intentional obstruction is not unheard of. The need thus is all the more clear for building international institutions with membership that follows logically from the task.

*Thomas D. Grant, "A League of Their Own: The Rationale for an International Alliance of Democracies,"* George Washington International Law Review, *vol. 41, no. 1, 2009.*

and the rule of law. This group includes the obvious candidates, such as the OECD [Organization for Economic Cooperation and Development] countries, but it also includes such nations as Botswana, Brazil, Costa Rica, India, Israel, Mauritius, Peru, the Philippines, and South Africa. In other words, the Concert of Democracies would be composed of a diverse group of countries from around the globe—small and large, rich and poor, North and South, strong and weak. Conversely, most countries around the world would not be eligible for membership, at least not initially. Countries on the outside looking in at a concert could become candidates over time once they embrace democratic values. Indeed, one of the purposes of the concert is to give autocracies incentives to embrace democratic practices. NATO [the North Atlantic Treaty Organization] and the European Union [EU] have served precisely this function in encouraging eastern European countries to democratize. For that reason, the concert must have provisions such that any country that meets basic democratic criteria can become a member.

## Incentives for Currently Eligible and Future Members

To deepen ties among democracies, the concert should seek to become a privileged trading group. By reducing tariffs and other trade barriers among its members, the concert would create a tangible economic premium for democratic rule that would not only benefit members but also provide concrete incentives for other states to become democracies. Traditional democracy promotion efforts founder because they require direct interventions in autocratic governments. Democracies channel funds to pro-democracy groups, or they demand that autocracies change their behavior. Smart autocrats exploit both types of policies to stoke nationalist sentiments and discredit democracy activists as agents of foreign powers. A strategy that seeks to lure autocracies toward democratic government avoids tarnishing democracy activists and rewards countries that choose the democratic path on their own. The EU's success with former Soviet bloc countries is illustrative on this score.

The idea of a Concert of Democracies has come under attack, especially since Senator John McCain championed it during his presidential campaign. The criticism is in many ways surprising. Democratic cooperation, after all, has long been at the heart of American foreign policy. NATO, the OECD, and bilateral security ties with such countries as Australia, Japan, and South Korea were never rooted in material or geopolitical interests alone. Rather, they are fundamentally based on and reflect shared democratic values, and they are by far our strongest ties by virtue of that fact. As successful as these arrangements have been, however, each is geographically confined, and none sees it as its mission to facilitate cooperation with the others. Most important, they all leave out emerging democratic powers, such as India, Brazil, and South Africa. By contrast, a Concert of Democracies offers the opportunity to recognize the changing global landscape and to engage new democratic partners.

## Cooperation Enables Success

But will these democracies want to work together? One criticism of the Concert of Democracies is that it rests on the illusion that "democracies share sufficient common interests to work effectively together." Of course, this complaint can be leveled against any large international institution—particularly those that critics of a Concert of Democracies prefer. The United Nations [UN] typically fails to bridge the differences among its members and, as a result, it usually endorses lowest-common-denominator actions or does nothing at all. Likewise, a "concert of great powers" that many so-called realists want to establish would inevitably founder over the fact that democracies and autocracies disagree not just on material interests but on the core values that should be embedded in the international system.

Democracies obviously are not immune to disagreement and discord. One has only to recall the transatlantic shouting match over Iraq in 2003 to see how bitterly they can disagree. But a Concert of Democracies does not depend on the mirage of common interests to succeed. Rather, it rests on two other premises. First, the world's democracies possess the greatest capacity to shape global politics: They deploy the greatest and most potent militaries, with the largest twenty democracies accounting for three-quarters of global defense spending. Democracies also account for most of the world's wealth, innovation, and productivity. Twenty-eight of the world's thirty largest economies are democracies. In the main, people living in democracies are better educated, more prosperous, healthier, and happier than the people who live in autocracies. Harnessing the power that comes from this overwhelming military, economic, political, and social advantage would provide the necessary ingredients for effective international action.

Second, democracies have a proven track record of bridging their differences and generating effective cooperation. Democracies work well together not just because they at times share common interests but because they share a commitment to the rule of law and the consent of the governed that enables them to trust one another. Intimidation and coercion are generally absent in their interactions. Conversely, relations between democracies and autocracies are always infused with suspicion and doubt. Will Russia respect the sovereignty of Georgia? Will China settle its differences with Taiwan peacefully? Democracies worry that the answer to these questions is "no" because autocracies often fail to keep their word.

What is most remarkable about democratic cooperation is that it has been achieved even though democracies are not in the habit, at least outside of the Atlantic Alliance, of thinking of themselves as a group. Brazilians think of the United States as a great power to the North. Italians think of Japan as an Asian power. Indians see Great Britain as a former colonial power. But the concert, by constructing a common identity among liberal democracies, will change how democracies interact and thereby further facilitate their cooperation.

## Making the UN More Effective

Would a Concert of Democracies push the United Nations onto the ash heap of history? Some proponents certainly hope so. And these hopes alarm those who see the United Nations as the last, best hope for humanity. Efforts to turn a Concert of Democracies into a substitute for the UN are destined to fail. Support for the UN is simply too deep and widespread. Just as important, efforts to use a Concert of Democracies to put the UN out of business *should* fail. By providing a forum where all the world's countries can participate, the UN serves a critical global function. Moreover, some of its specialized agencies, such as the UN High Commissioner for Refugees, the World Food Programme, and the World Health Organization, provide important services. Even the UN's most ardent supporters, however, admit that the organization on the whole does not work terribly well. Ban Ki-moon admitted as much upon becoming secretary-general when he promised to fix things during his tenure. His initial appointments and actions, though, hardly suggest significant change. Indeed, several decades of failed reform attempts make clear that a majority of UN members prefer the status quo, however imperfect it may be, and actively resist reform—radical or otherwise.

A robust Concert of Democracies would change that calculation. Just as in private business, international institutions benefit from competition. If the concert becomes effective at mobilizing cooperation, the UN will feel pressure to do likewise—or watch itself become irrelevant. Indeed, the concert could make UN reform one of its top priorities. As one of its first steps it should create a "D-60" to join the ranks of the P-5 [the five permanent members of the UN security council] and the G-8 [the governments of eight major international economies] to push for change at the United Nations. This would highlight the reality that a Concert of Democracies is not intended to replace the UN but to spur it to become more effective.

## A New Cold War Will Not Begin

Could a Concert of Democracies succeed if it excludes powerful countries, such as China and Russia? Of course it could.

Many successful international organizations do not count China and Russia as members. Neither country belongs to NATO, the European Union, or the Organization for Economic Cooperation and Development. China does not belong to the G-8, and Russia stands (at least for now) outside the World Trade Organization. No one argues that these institutions are ineffective because their memberships are not universal. Again, the purpose of the Concert of Democracies is not to replace or supplant all other international institutions. A major part of its mission is to push, persuade, and cajole other international institutions as well as autocratic governments into taking action.

A related worry is that a Concert of Democracies could trigger a new cold war. Chinese and Russian leaders might view the concert as an effort to encircle and constrain them. Even if they do not respond by erecting a new iron curtain, they might refuse to cooperate with the concert on matters of mutual interest, or so the argument goes. Beijing and Moscow will no doubt denounce the formation of a Concert of Democracies. After all, the concert's purpose is to forge a global order conducive to democratic political principles and hostile to autocratic ones. But why should democracies take their cues on permissible forms of cooperation from autocracies? Beijing and Moscow show no similar deference to democracies. From Asia to Africa to the Americas, they have aggressively sought to use their economic and military strength to shape the global order to suit their own interests at the expense of others.

This is not to say that the effort to create a Concert of Democracies will not require careful diplomacy. It will. It is to say that the dangers of alienating Beijing and Moscow are greatly overstated. To begin with, any attempt by Washington to use the concert to isolate China and Russia is pointless. There is no surer way to render the concert stillborn than to make it a vehicle for containing either country. Other democracies simply will not follow Washington's lead. By the same token, it is wrong to assume that just because Beijing and Moscow denounce a concert they will refuse to work with it. As realist thinkers have long preached, states act to advance their interests; they do not cut off their noses to spite their faces. Beijing and Moscow will cooperate on climate change and international financial issues when they see it in their interest to do so, not because democracies have declined to work together.

Most important, complaints that a Concert of Democracies will trigger a new cold war rest on an unpersuasive binary logic: Democracies either can work to advance their common interests and values or they can work with non-democracies. But no democracy faces this choice. They can do both. All major democracies, including the United States, have extensive public and private ties to all major authoritarian states. That is not going to change, and it should not change. If anything, the United States and other countries seeking to create a concert should individually and collectively work to improve their relations with autocratic governments. Bilateral relations can be strengthened; regional initiatives can be launched; and, perhaps most obviously, China can be invited to join the G-8.

## Multiple Partnerships Foster Greater Cooperation

The broader point is that the case for a Concert of Democracies is not axiomatically a case against great power cooperation or bilateral collaboration or regional relationships. We can and should try to create multiple partnerships. Indeed, in an age of globalization, attempts to craft a single venue for cooperation are futile. We are likely to be far better served by what [American philosopher and political economist] Francis Fukuyama has called "multi-multilateralisms." These overlapping and cross-cutting political networks are not only more likely to generate cooperation by creating new forums for action, they are also likely to make the international community far more durable and stable than one with only a few fault lines because they blur sharp divisions and create opportunities to build new coalitions.

A Concert of Democracies will not magically solve global ills. It will not emerge on the international scene fully formed like Botticelli's Venus. Just as the European Union began with the small (in retrospect) step of coordinating coal and steel production and then took four decades to reach the point of creating a common currency, a concert will take time to build. It is most likely to succeed if its members begin with manageable challenges, such as developing a common agenda for reforming international institutions and coordinating their development programs. It is least likely to succeed—indeed, it is likely to fail—if it begins with the most difficult and controversial challenges, such as humanitarian intervention.

The task at hand is daunting. But before despairing over the work that needs to be done, it is worth asking if we can afford not to deepen democratic cooperation. The failure to bring democracies together will not mean sustaining an acceptable status quo; it will mean continued inadequate and ineffective responses to the many problems that now transcend international borders. If we do not press forward, we will fall back. That is our real choice.

> *"Fashioning a peaceful order for the twenty-first century will require navigating a two-way street; the West cannot just make a take-it-or-leave-it offer."*

# A League of Democracies Would Not Benefit the World nor Spread Democracy

*Charles A. Kupchan*

*In the viewpoint that follows, Charles A. Kupchan seeks to discredit the notion that a league of democracies will benefit both its members and its nonmembers and will work as a force to spread peace, democracy, and prosperity around the world. In this argument, he contends that such a league not only is unnecessary in ensuring the continued cooperation of the world's democracies but would create a sharp divide between democracies and autocracies, making cooperation among such countries even more unlikely. The author blends both historical and contemporary examples to support this view and comes to the conclusion that a league would do more harm than good. Charles A. Kupchan is an international affairs professor at Georgetown University and a senior fellow at the Council on Foreign Relations.*

Charles A. Kupchan, "Minor League, Major Problems," *Foreign Affairs*, vol. 87, no. 6, November-December, 2008. Reprinted by permission of FOREIGN AFFAIRS, November-December. Copyright 2008 by the Council on Foreign Relations, Inc. www.ForeignAffairs.com. All rights reserved. Reproduced by permission.

As you read, consider the following questions:

1. The author does not believe that a league of democracies can exist and also foster cooperation with autocracies; what does he see as the two possibilities of what could happen?

2. What historic examples of cooperation between democracies and autocracies does the author cite to show the common interests between countries with these two forms of government?

3. According to the author, in what ways would legitimacy of the league be a problem?

The call to establish a "league of democracies" was one of the hottest policy proposals this past election season [2008]. Advocates contended that creating a club open exclusively to the world's liberal democracies would enhance the ability of like-minded states to address the challenges of the twenty-first century. Not since the 1940s, when the United States orchestrated the founding of the United Nations [UN] and the Bretton Woods monetary system, have voices on both sides of the aisle called for such an ambitious overhaul of international institutions. Influential advisers to both Senator Barack Obama (D-Ill.) and Senator John McCain (R-Ariz.) enthusiastically backed the proposal, and McCain explicitly endorsed the idea. "Rarely," as the journalist Jonathan Rauch has observed, "have liberal idealism and neoconservative realism converged so completely."

The proposal to launch a league of democracies has its merits. The size and diversity of the UN's membership hinder the organization's ability to coordinate timely and effective action. And whether the task at hand is containing Iran's nuclear program or stopping genocide in Darfur, China and Russia regularly block action by the UN Security Council. In contrast, liberal democracies are generally prepared to work together to pursue common interests. When it comes to political will, economic resources, and military strength, the world's democracies constitute a uniquely fraternal grouping of states.

Nonetheless, the next occupant of the White House should shelve the idea of establishing a league of democracies. Such a club is not needed to secure cooperation among liberal democracies—they are already regular partners—and it would draw new lines between democracies and non-democracies, thus compromising their relations just when adapting the international system to the rise of illiberal powers is becoming a paramount challenge. Contrary to the expectations of its advocates, moreover, a league would expose the limits of the West's power and appeal, revealing the constraints on solidarity among democracies, eroding the legitimacy of the West, and arresting the global spread of democracy. With its marginal upsides and dramatic downsides, establishing a league of democracies would not be a wise investment for the next president, whose time and political capital will be severely taxed by an economic downturn at home and abroad and by conflict in the Middle East. . . .

## Democracies Should Focus on Cooperating with Autocracies

The case for creating a league of democracies does not fare well under closer scrutiny. Most important, a global forum that denies autocracies a say in world affairs promises to deepen cooperation where it is least needed (among democracies that are already reliable collaborators) at the expense of cooperation where it is most needed (between democracies and non-democracies). After decades of working together in a thick network of institutions, such as NATO [North Atlantic Treaty Organization], the EU [European Union], and the U.S.-Japanese security pact, many of the world's democracies have become trusted partners. It is this tested bond that makes the notion of a league of democracies appealing—and unnecessary. An initiative that ekes out only a marginal increase in cooperation among already close allies does not merit being the centerpiece of U.S. foreign policy.

Instead, the United States and its democratic allies should invest in greater collaboration with rising autocracies, such as China, Russia, and the oil-rich states of the Persian Gulf. Democratic teamwork will not be enough to meet today's challenges. Shutting down nuclear programs in Iran and North Korea, fighting terrorism, curbing global warming, managing energy supplies, and building regional security orders in East Asia and the Persian Gulf will require the help of illiberal regimes. Guiding democracies and non-democracies toward common ground and instilling the habits of cooperation between them are unquestionably more urgent than topping off solidarity among democracies.

Advocates of a league respond that closer cooperation among democracies need not come at the expense of their relationships with autocratic states. The national interests of China, Russia, and other illiberal regimes will compel them to work with the league, the theory goes, and the interests of democracies will induce them to reciprocate. "Our national interests," McCain argues, "require that we pursue economic and strategic cooperation with China and Russia, that we support Egypt and Saudi Arabia's role as peacemakers in the Middle East, and that we work with Pakistan to fight the Taliban and al Qaeda." But this assertion is a hedge. . . .

The league's supporters cannot have it both ways—maintaining that the new body would bring momentous benefits to the cause of international cooperation while insisting that its negative side effects would be minimal. Either the organization is, like Bill Clinton's Community of Democracies, little more than a salon, or it meets the high expectations of its supporters and deliberately excludes autocracies from the inner sanctum of international politics, thereby encouraging them to chart their own course. Russia's blustery reactions to the enlargement of NATO and Kosovo's independence from Serbia, its forceful intervention in Georgia this past summer, and its teamwork with China to form the Shanghai Cooperation Organization are a hint of what might lie in store. The author Robert Kagan argues that a "league of dictators" is already taking shape, which is precisely the reason, in his view, that democracies must respond in kind. Kagan's concern is premature, but the surest way to turn it into reality would be to fashion an alliance of democracies—against which illiberal states would be quick to balance.

## Historic Cooperation Between Democracies and Autocracies

Advocates of a league both underestimate the potential for cooperation between democracies and autocracies and overestimate the scope of common interests among democracies. These misconceptions appear to stem at least in part from a misreading of recent history. McCain pines for the "vital democratic solidarity" of the Cold War and sees a league of democracies as a way to revive it. But yesterday's solidarity was the product of an alliance against an external threat, not of an alignment based exclusively on regime type. Although advocates of a league often treat Presidents Franklin Roosevelt and Harry Truman as standard-bearers for their cause, both leaders envisaged a post–World War II order in which the great powers—whether democracies or not—would collectively manage the international system. Roosevelt wanted to establish the "Four Policeman," a global directorate comprising the United States, the United Kingdom, the Soviet Union, and China. This concept informed the design of the UN Security Council, with China and the Soviet Union included as permanent, veto-wielding members—hardly a club of democracies.

Roosevelt's preference for a great-power concert was based on realism, not naiveté. During the 1930s, France and the United Kingdom eschewed an alliance with the Soviet Union—primarily for ideological reasons. Had Paris and London instead allowed strategic prudence to override their antipathy toward communism, World War II may well have been avoided, or at least shortened. Indeed, it was the alliance between the Soviet Union and the liberal democracies of the West that ultimately defeated Nazi Germany and imperial Japan.

Not until the late 1940s, after it had become clear that the United States and the Soviet Union would be strategic rivals, did U.S. leaders abandon hopes of fashioning a cooperative postwar order and instead erect a network of alliances that set many of the world's democracies against the communist bloc. Still, through-out the Cold War, the United States maintained close partnerships with a host of unsavory regimes. China's government may have been autocratic and communist, but that did not deter President Richard Nixon from reaching out to Beijing, a move that signifi-cantly altered the course of the Cold War and helped set China on a path toward liberalization. Washington continues to work closely with autocracies even in the absence of the strategic imperatives of the Cold War rivalry. As long as the United States has troops in Iraq and an economy dependent on oil from the Persian Gulf, it will maintain strong ties with Bahrain, Qatar, and the United Arab Emirates—some of the most illiberal countries on the planet.

## All Democracies Do Not Have the Same Interests

Much as they underestimate the potential for cooperation be-tween democracies and autocracies, proponents of a league over-state the ease of cooperation among democratic states. Although they have similar domestic systems, democracies often have diverging interests. In seeking to block the invasion of Iraq in 2003, for example, France and Germany broke with the United States on fundamental questions of war and peace. NATO, de-spite almost 60 years of experience, is struggling to maintain its unity. At the alliance's 2008 summit in Bucharest, Washington pressed for putting Georgia and Ukraine on the road to mem-bership—only to have the move rejected by its European allies. In Afghanistan, the solidarity of NATO is being sorely strained by stipulations restricting the participation of most national contingents to peacekeeping and reconstruction. The same goes for the EU, whose members have struggled to maintain a consensus on sanctions against Iran and failed to agree on whether to recognize an independent Kosovo.

If NATO and the EU, which are essentially miniature leagues of democracies with track records decades long, are confronting such tribulations, it is hard to see how creating a bigger club of democracies would make things better. The more global the organization, the more likely regional considerations will trump democratic solidarity. South Africa is a democracy, but its recent coddling of Robert Mugabe, the Zimbabwean leader who clubbed his way to reelection, is a case in point. Latin America now counts many democracies, but most of them want nothing to do with U.S. efforts to isolate Cuba.

Not only are free and fair elections no guarantee of cooperation among democracies, but they also can impede it. The EU is perhaps the quintessential zone of democratic peace, but recent referendums in France, the Netherlands, and Ireland rejected institutional reforms aimed at tightening the bonds among the union's members. China may have contributed to the collapse of the Doha Round of international trade talks this past summer, but at least as important was the stalemate between the United States and India—two democracies mindful of powerful economic interest groups at home.

## The Lack of Legitimacy

A league is likely to lack legitimacy not just among autocracies but also among Europe's democracies, for whom approval from the UN Security Council is the litmus test of legitimate action. As [British journalist] Gideon Rachman has written in the *Financial Times*, "Almost all of America's closest democratic allies have deep reservations about a league of democracies. The Europeans are committed to the UN and would be loath to join an alliance that undermined it."

European objections aside, advocates of a league are on shaky ground when they argue that international legitimacy derives primarily from democratic governments. If democracies are legitimate because they represent the will of their citizens, could a global body that spoke for less than half the world's population and represented less than one-third of the world's nations ever be considered legitimate? Should China's 1.3 billion citizens be doubly disenfranchised—no voice abroad as well as no democracy at home?

Such logical tensions would weigh heavily on the league's standing. A recent study commissioned by the UN concluded that its personnel are increasingly targets of attacks because of the organization's perceived bias in favor of its most powerful members. If the UN has such credibility problems, the league's, as the *New York Times*' James Traub has pointed out, would be far more acute. Consider its potential engagement in the Middle East, a region that would probably have two members in the global body—Israel and Turkey—but no Arab representatives. Were the league to carry out a military intervention in the region, the Arab world would see it as the West against the rest—and react with even more hostility than it did to the 2003 invasion of Iraq. . . .

Finally, it is likely that establishing a league of democracies would do more to tarnish the international reputation of liberal democracy than it would to burnish it. At present, the world's major democracies can blame their own inaction on the UN'S structural deficiencies and the stiff-necked autocracies that populate the Security Council. China and Russia are the regular culprits; they are responsible for blocking tougher measures against Iran and Sudan, for example. But the Europeans, concerned about the economic and diplomatic consequences of more stringent sanctions against Tehran, are quietly relieved that Moscow is taking the heat for resisting U.S. pressure. Although China may not be particularly helpful in confronting the Sudanese government, the main impediment to Western military action in Darfur is not the UN; it is the reluctance of the United States and its democratic allies to assume the costs and risks of intervention. Were a league of democracies unwilling to act, and the UN unavailable to take the blame, liberal democracies alone would have to bear the moral burden. The world's democracies had better deliberate carefully before taking on pledges to engage in joint action that they may well fail to honor—thus exposing the fragility of democratic solidarity.

## Misunderstanding the Spread of Democracy

Drawing on the success of NATO and the EU in spreading democracy in Europe, the league's proponents contend that the prospect of joining the new body would encourage illiberal regimes around the world to democratize. But the league would not enjoy a magnetic appeal comparable to the Atlantic institutions. In central and eastern Europe, the peoples that had long suffered under Soviet rule yearned for inclusion in the democratic West in the aftermath of the Cold War—in no small part to gain protection against the potential resurgence of Russian ambition. In contrast, Moscow and Beijing, rather than looking for outside help with political reform, are dead set against a rapid transition to liberal democracy. They also tend to see the West as more of a threat than an answer to their security concerns. Moscow has already emerged as the leading challenger to the West's primacy, taking on NATO and the EU over the independence of Kosovo, the status of Georgia's breakaway regions of Abkhazia and South Ossetia, missile defense in Europe, Iran's nuclear program, and a host of other issues. Meanwhile, Beijing is busy building a multilateral framework in East Asia that seems intended to displace the United States as the hub of the region's security order. Both Russia and China are taking their own roads instead of following the West's lead, a dynamic that would only be reinforced by the new geopolitical dividing lines that a league of democracies would draw.

Plans to make the league a privileged trading group, another element of the proposal, also promise to alienate countries that do not initially make the grade. According to McCain, the body would offer market access exclusively to countries that "share the values of economic and political freedom." But such conditionality would undercut a key plank of the logic of democratization—namely, that trade helps nurture a middle class, which is itself a building block of political reform. The league would enhance the prosperity of Norway when it is Pakistan and other illiberal countries that need access to developed markets.

Confidence about the league's ability to spread liberal democracy to the rest of the world reveals a deeper misunderstanding of the nature of the historical moment. Such optimism is predicated on the belief that the world is now at a way station on the road to democracy; that the West provides the sole viable model of development for nations around the world; that China, Russia, and their kindred spirits are the last holdouts but are soon to join the march of history; and that the league is meant to help them complete their transition. But the world is far from arriving at such a historical endpoint; it is heading toward continued diversity, not greater homogeneity.

## Enabling Diverse Coalitions

McCain contends that today's illiberal regimes are "trying to rebuild nineteenth-century autocracies in a twenty-first-century world." They are not; they are building twenty-first-century autocracies. Sustained rates of economic growth and the surge in national wealth enjoyed by energy producers will give many of the world's autocracies remarkable staying power. China, Russia, and the oil-soaked sheikdoms of the Persian Gulf are co-opting and buying off their middle classes, not pursuing democratic reforms. Oil wealth, which accounts for 60 percent of Iran's national budget, may well underwrite the theocratic regime in Tehran for some time to come. Meanwhile, economic performance in the United States and Europe is poised to lag well behind that in China and Russia for the foreseeable future. China now holds about $500 billion of the United States' massive debt, roughly 20 percent of the total, and sovereign wealth funds from the Persian Gulf states are snapping up U.S. assets.

For now, state-led, authoritarian capitalism has at least as much appeal in many quarters of the globe as the democratic alternative. It should come as no surprise that a recent global survey of public opinion ranked Russian Prime Minister Vladimir Putin and Chinese President Hu Jintao among the world's most highly regarded leaders. Another survey revealed that 86 percent of Chinese citizens polled were content with their country's direction, compared with 23 percent of Americans with the United States.

The idea that a league of democracies would represent a pact for perpetual peace into which the rest of the world would soon enter is illusory. The liberal international order erected by the West may suit its founder, the United States, and its junior partners, but one size does not fit all. If a new global order is to emerge, Washington and Brussels will have to adjust to the preferences of rising autocracies, just as Beijing and Moscow have had to adjust to the West. Fashioning a peaceful order for the twenty-first century will require navigating a two-way street; the West cannot just make a take-it-or-leave-it offer. If the liberal democracies fail to understand that the coming world will be both multi-polar and politically diverse, they will be heading down a dead end—not, as they hope, blazing a path to the end of history.

# Periodical Bibliography

*The following articles have been selected to supplement the diverse views presented in this chapter.*

Mike Albertus and Victor Menaldo — "For Enduring Democracies, Revolutions Are Best Bet," *USA Today*, March 2, 2011.

Kai Bird — "America's 'Shah' in Egypt," *The Nation*, February 21, 2011.

Maya Rockeymoore Cummings — "Mubarak Steps Down: Obama's a Big Reason Why," *Christian Science Monitor*, February 11, 2011.

Christopher Hayes — "Discomfited by Democracy," *The Nation*, February 28, 2011.

Daniel Henninger — "Is U.S. Democracy Just Talk?," *Wall Street Journal*, March 10, 2011.

Bobby Jindal — "A Stronger America Means a Safer World," *Human Events*, December 13, 2010.

James Kitfield — "Democracy Stalled," *National Journal*, May 3, 2008.

Monty G. Marshall — "The New Democratic Order," *Harvard International Review*, Spring 2011.

Rachelle Marshall — "Democracy May Be Good for Egyptians, But Not for Palestinians," *Washington Report on Middle East Affairs*, April 2011.

Lincoln A. Mitchell — "Democracy Bound," *National Interest*, May-June 2008.

Joshua Muravchik — "The Abandonment of Democracy," *Commentary*, July-August 2009.

*New Republic* — "The Lessons of Cairo," March 3, 2011.

Justin Raimondo — "Gang of Democracies," *American Conservative*, October 6, 2008.

Robert Spencer — "Obama's Democracy Delusions," *Human Events*, March 2011.

# For Further Discussion

## Chapter 1

1. Reexamine the arguments made in the first two viewpoints of this chapter. What rhetorical strategies does Anwar Ibrahim utilize to make his claim that democratic values are taking hold in Asia? What evidence does *The Economist* give to suggest that liberal democracy is in "intellectual retreat"? Whose argument do you find more compelling? Explain why you sided with one author over the other.

2. After rereading Michael Mandelbaum's viewpoint, explain why he believes free markets help countries see the benefits of democracy. Specifically, what ideals does Mandelbaum think are shared by democracy and free trade? Why does Robert B. Reich disagree with this argument? According to Reich, what ideals does capitalism espouse that are not shared by democracy? Do you see a connection between free markets and democracy? Explain why or why not while referring to the given arguments.

3. The Internet has been touted as a means to bring together dissident voices in countries that are ruled by oppressive regimes. For example, following elections in Iran (2009–2010) and civil uprisings in Tunisia (2010–2011) and Egypt (2011), global news media reported on the ways in which the people of these countries were connecting to each other and to people outside their borders via up-to-the-minute posts on Twitter. The media created the phrase "Twitter revolution" to connote how this interconnectivity could potentially lead to more coordinated struggles for democracy in such lands. Looking back at the last two viewpoints in this chapter and doing some research on the outcomes of Twitter revolutions, do you think the Internet is a tool of democracy? Explain.

# Chapter 2

1. After rereading the viewpoints in this chapter and doing any outside research you can, describe what obstacles you believe exist to the spread of democracy in Arab and Islamic countries. Do you think these obstacles can be overcome or at least that Islamic nations can have free governments? Explain why or why not.

2. After reading the viewpoints by James Phillips, David M. Faris and Stacey Philbrick Yadav, and Maajid Nawaz, explain what role you think the Muslim Brotherhood has in creating a new Egyptian government in the wake of Hosni Mubarak's resignation. What arguments would make you believe the Brotherhood would resist democracy? What arguments lead you to believe the Brotherhood would not stand in the way of democratic change? Whose claims do you find most convincing? Explain why.

3. Jacob Dayan claims that Israel is a true democracy because it tolerates voices of dissent and because it makes its public services (e.g., transport and education) available to all citizens regardless of their heritage. Josh Ruebner makes the opposite argument, insisting that Israel is a divided society with Jews on top and Arab citizens on the bottom. He asserts that Arabs are constantly harassed and their loyalty is always under suspicion. After reading these viewpoints, do you think Israel is a democracy or an ethnocracy?

# Chapter 3

1. The authors of the first two viewpoints in this chapter examine the current state of the US democratic system, arguing that it is either damaged and unable to function properly, as stated by Eric Alterman, or that is it thriving and functioning as well as ever, as T.A. Barnhart contends. Alterman focuses his critique on the shortcomings of the institutions within the government, such as the rules gov-

erning the Senate, while Barnhart focuses his praise on examples of the American people's participation in the democratic process. Which of these arguments do you find more convincing? In your opinion, where does the strength of the US democracy lie? Is it in the government itself or is it with the citizens?

2. Viewpoints 3, 4, and 5 in this chapter focus on how the US tax code should be changed to improve US democracy. Do you agree with these authors that the tax code affects the democratic system and citizens' participation in the government? Explain why or why not. Now, reread each viewpoint and determine which tax code reform you believe would be the most conducive to advancing US democracy, if any. Support your answer using quotes from the text, or outside sources if you think that none of these solutions is necessary or best.

3. The final viewpoints in Chapter 3 present two views of the potential impact of the January 2010 US Supreme Court decision *Citizens United v. Federal Election Commission*. Conduct some outside research and find the majority and dissenting opinions on these cases. Read through both and decide whether you think the Supreme Court made the correct decision in allowing corporations to fund political advertisements. Do you think the First Amendment to the US Constitution protects the free speech rights of corporations just as it does for people? Should corporations be allowed the same rights as people in this case? Use quotes from the justices' opinions to support your view.

## Chapter 4

1. Shadi Hamid and Steven Brooke argue that US promotion of democracy worldwide increases national security. Michael S. Rozeff disagrees. Look back over these two viewpoints, then conduct outside research to determine the current situa-

tion in two countries where the United States has embarked on democracy promotion efforts. Have US efforts in these places been successful? Give examples to support your argument.

2. The United States has focused much of its democracy promotion efforts in recent years on the Middle East. Beginning in December 2010, people from countries across this region began to rise up against oppressive regimes with calls for democratic change spreading from Tunisia to Egypt, Libya, Syria, Yemen, and Bahrain. After reading viewpoints 3 and 4, what role do you think the United States should take in the Middle East in response to these democratic uprisings? Should the country support the people who are leading these calls for democracy even if their views of the United States are negative? Use support from the viewpoints to back up your claims.

3. In recent years, some government leaders have presented the idea that the creation of a "league of democracies "would help democratic governments worldwide advance their positions in the international society and spread democratic ideals by providing incentives to adopt this form of governance. James M. Lindsay supports this view; however, Charles A. Kupchan argues that this proposed league would create more problems than it would solve. Which argument do you agree with? Do you think a league of democracies would benefit the world, or would it only create more divisions? Do you think there is a better way to join democracies together and promote the widespread adoption of democracy? Is this a goal that countries should be striving to achieve? Include quotes from the viewpoints when explaining your stance.

# Organizations to Contact

*The editors have compiled the following list of organizations concerned with the issues debated in this book. The descriptions are derived from materials provided by the organizations. All have publications or information available for interested readers. The list was compiled on the date of publication of the present volume; the information provided here may change. Be aware that many organizations take several weeks or longer to respond to inquiries, so allow as much time as possible.*

**American Enterprise Institute (AEI)**
1150 Seventeenth Street NW
Washington, DC 20036
(202) 862-5800 • fax: (202) 862-7177
website: www.aei.org

AEI is an organization that provides an opportunity for scholars and experts in all areas of public policy to research and debate current issues facing the United States and the international community. Most of the research is focused in six areas—economics, foreign policy and defense, health policy, legal and constitutional issues, politics and public opinion, and social and cultural studies. The organization's publications generally espouse support for the promotion of democracy as the best means of government as well as a method of ensuring US national security. Articles explicating these views can be found on the AEI website along with back issues of the organization's monthly publication *The American*.

**Brookings Institution**
1775 Massachusetts Ave. NW
Washington, DC 20036
(202) 797-6000
website: www.brookings.edu

Brookings is a nonprofit organization dedicated to researching public policy issues concerning the United States and then using the findings to offer policy suggestions that improve American democracy, ensure that all Americans enjoy economic and social well-being, and advance international relations to a safer and more collaborative state. With such goals, the organization's focus on democracy spans from the local to the global, and numerous articles and reports have been written on democracy building and governance. The institute has also held conferences to gather top experts in the field to discuss the possibilities for democracy promotion worldwide. Information about these events and publications can be found on the organization's website.

### Carnegie Endowment for International Peace

1779 Massachusetts Ave. NW
Washington, DC 20036-2103
(202) 483-7600 • fax: (202) 483-1840
e-mail: info@carnegieendowment.org
website: www.carnegieendowment.org

Founded in 1910, the Carnegie Endowment for International Peace, a private, nonprofit organization, seeks to further cooperation between nations around the globe and encourage the United States to remain an active participant in international relations. The organization monitors democracy promotion efforts made by Western powers as well as internal efforts by local actors to enact democratic change. Papers such as "Challenges to Democracy Promotion: The Case of Bolivia" and "Middle East Democracy Is Not a One-way Street" can be accessed on the Carnegie Endowment website.

### Cato Institute

1000 Massachusetts Ave. NW
Washington, DC 20001-5403
(202) 842-0200 • fax: (202) 842-3490
website: www.cato.org

Cato is a libertarian think tank seeking to promote ideals such as individual liberty, limited government, free markets, and peace. In its work on public policy issues including democracy, Cato commissions research, sponsors conferences, and publishes numerous materials on related issues. Publications on democracy range from the state of democracy in the United States to the promotion and expansion of democracy worldwide and include titles such as "Globalization, Human Rights and Democracy," and "Trade, Democracy, and Peace: The Virtuous Cycle." These articles and others can be read on the Cato website along with digital copies of Cato publications such as the *Cato Journal, Cato Policy Report*, and *Cato's Letters*.

### Democracy Unlimited of Humboldt County (DUHC)
PO Box 610
Eureka, CA 95502-0610
(707) 269-0984
website: www.democracyunlimited.ning.com

Based in Humboldt County, California, DUHC works at local and national levels to inform people about what it sees as the ever-increasing corporate control over the US government, a circumstance it asserts has decreased the people's say in how the government is run. The organization seeks to promote action on a grassroots level and motivate the citizens of the United States to take back their government and fight corporate rule. The DUHC website provides an article titled "The Hidden History of Corporate Rule" as well as videos on related topics and a catalog of relevant books available in the organization's library on social change.

### Heritage Foundation
214 Massachusetts Ave. NE
Washington, DC 20002-4999
(202) 546-4400
e-mail: info@heritage.org
website: www.heritage.org

The Heritage Foundation is a public policy institute whose research espouses the conservative ideals of free enterprise, limited government, individual freedom, traditional American values, and a strong national defense. As such the organization is dedicated to exploring the effects of current legislation on the American democratic system as well as the possibilities for democracy promotion worldwide. Reports such as "Championing Liberty Abroad to Counter Islamist Extremism" and "Soft Despotism, Democracy's Drift: What Tocqueville Teaches Today," can be read online.

## International Institute for Democracy and Electoral Assistance (IDEA)
International IDEA
Strömsborg SE-103 34
Stockholm, Sweden
+46 8 698 3700 • fax: +46 8 20 24 22
website: www.idea.int

An intergovernmental organization, International IDEA seeks to foster the expansion of democracy worldwide through a concerted effort that consists of education, assistance, and influence as the main strategies employed to create sustainable democracies around the world. The organization's main areas of expertise include electoral processes, constitution building processes, political parties, participation and representation, and democracy and development. Information about International IDEA's current projects as well as current publications such as "The Financial and Economic Crisis: Some Implications for Democracy Building," "Effective Democracy Assistance," and "Democracy in the 21st Century: Advance or Decline?" can be accessed on the organization's website.

## National Democratic Institute (NDI)
2030 M Street NW
Fifth Floor

Washington, DC 20036-3306
(202) 728-5500 • fax: (202) 728-5520
website: www.ndi.org

NDI has been working since its founding in 1983 to create and improve democratic governments, elections, and citizen participation in more than 100 countries around the world. The institute provides support to its partners by fostering the exchange of information between individuals with expertise in democracy building and those who are looking to implement the process of change in their own countries. Information about the countries within which NDI operates as well as the organization's partner groups can be found online along with access to publications on individual countries and regions and their development as democracies.

**Project on Middle East Democracy (POMED)**
1820 Jefferson Place NW, Suite 400
Washington, DC 20036
(202) 828-9660
website: www.pomed.org

POMED employs dialogue, research, and advocacy in an attempt to determine how to foster the growth of democratic governments in the Middle East and to define the United States' role in that endeavor. To implement this three-pronged approach, the organization sponsors conferences, panel discussions, and working groups; researches and publishes findings for legislators and organizations that promote democratic rule; and seeks to establish a US foreign policy toward the Middle East with democracy promotion as a main tenet. Organization publications such as "After Cairo: From the Vision of the Cairo Speech to Active Support for Human Dignity" and "Strategies for Engaging Political Islam" can be read on the POMED website.

## ReclaimDemocracy.org

222 S. Black Ave.
Bozeman, MT 59715
(406) 582-1224
e-mail: info@ReclaimDemocracy.org
website: www.reclaimdemocracy.org

ReclaimDemocracy.org is a nonpartisan, nonprofit organization that encourages citizens to take a more active role in shaping US democracy and government and restricting the influence of corporations on this process. The organization works to educate the public, implement constitutional change and the reversal of Supreme Court precedents, establish change from the grassroots level, and redefine the language used to discuss relevant issues. Information on topics such as corporate personhood, independent business, transforming politics, and Wal-Mart, among others, is available on ReclaimDemocracy.org.

## United States Institute of Peace (USIP)

2301 Constitution Ave. NW
Washington, DC 20037
(202) 457-1700 • fax: (202) 429-6063
website: www.usip.org

Believing that the United States plays a crucial role in achieving peace worldwide, USIP takes an active role in creating the guidelines and tools necessary to ready peace-builders for the multiple tasks of preventing and ending conflict, establishing stability, and fostering professional standards for peace-building as a field. The institute is active with individuals from the international community in providing education and assistance to accomplish its goal of world peace. Publications concerning the role of democracy promotion in this process can be read online, including titles such as "In Pursuit of Democracy and Security in the Greater Middle East" and "Islam and Democracy."

**World Movement for Democracy (WMD)**
1025 F Street NW, Suite 800
Washington, DC 20004
(202) 378-9700
e-mail: world@ned.org
website: www.wmd.org

WMD unites advocates from around the world in a coalition seeking to promote the spread of the democratic form of governance. Founded by the National Endowment for Democracy in partnership with a global assembly in New Delhi, India, the group has been working since 1999 to aid pro-democracy groups in transitioning other forms of government into democracies. The two main projects currently being implemented by the organization include Defending Civil Society and Democracy Assistance. Information about these missions as well as others—such as protecting journalists, enhancing political participation of traditionally marginalized groups, and exploring the role of the Internet and technology in democracy promotion—can be found online.

**World Youth Movement for Democracy (WYMD)**
e-mail: info@wymdonline.org
website: www.wymdonline.org

WYMD is the youth branch of the World Movement for Democracy and provides a forum for young democracy activists to interact, exchange ideas, build solidarity, and give youth a voice in the spread of democracy worldwide. A monthly newsletter provides current information about the organization's ongoing activities, the challenges faced by youth activists, and accomplishments in the movement, as well as details about how interested individuals can become involved.

# Bibliography of Books

Eric Alterman

*Kabuki Democracy: The System vs. Barack Obama.* New York: Nation, 2011.

Larry M. Bartels

*Unequal Democracy: The Political Economy of the New Gilded Age.* Princeton, NJ: Princeton University Press, 2010.

Bruce Bimber

*Information and American Democracy: Technology in the Evolution of Political Power.* New York: Cambridge University Press, 2003.

Thomas Carothers

*Critical Mission: Essays on Democracy Promotion.* Washington, DC: Carnegie Endowment for International Peace, 2004.

Angelo M. Codevilla

*The Ruling Class: How They Corrupted America and What We Can Do About It.* New York: Beaufort, 2010.

Paul Collier

*Wars, Guns, and Votes: Democracy in Dangerous Places.* New York: HarperCollins, 2009.

Robert A. Dahl

*On Democracy.* New Haven, CT: Yale University Press, 2000.

Larry Diamond

*The Spirit of Democracy: The Struggle to Build Free Societies Throughout the World.* New York: Henry Holt, 2008.

| John Dunn | *Democracy: A History*. New York: Atlantic Monthly, 2005. |
| --- | --- |
| Matthew Hindman | *The Myth of Digital Democracy*. Princeton, NJ: Princeton University Press, 2009. |
| Samuel P. Huntington | *The Third Wave: Democratization in the Late Twentieth Century*. Norman: University of Oklahoma Press, 1991. |
| John Keane | *The Life and Death of Democracy*. New York: Norton, 2009. |
| John Markoff | *Waves of Democracy: Social Movements and Political Change*. Thousand Oaks, CA: Pine Forge, 1996. |
| Michael McFaul | *Advancing Democracy Abroad: Why We Should and How We Can*. Lanham, MD: Rowman & Littlefield, 2010. |
| Kenneth Minogue | *The Servile Mind: How Democracy Erodes the Moral Life*. New York: Encounter, 2010. |
| Barrington Moore Jr. | *Social Origins of Dictatorship and Democracy: Lord and Peasant in the Making of the Modern World*. Reprint edition. Boston: Beacon, 1993. |
| Joshua Muravchik | *The Next Founders: Voices of Democracy in the Middle East*. New York: Encounter, 2009. |
| Walid Phares | *The Coming Revolution: Struggle for Freedom in the Middle East*. New York: Threshold, 2010. |

Richard A. Posner *The Crisis of Capitalist Democracy*. Cambridge, MA: Harvard University Press, 2010.

Dani Rodrik *The Globalization Paradox: Democracy and the Future of the World Economy*. New York: Norton, 2011.

Natan Sharansky with Ron Dermer *The Case for Democracy: The Power of Freedom to Overcome Tyranny and Terror*. New York: Public Affairs, 2006.

Vandana Shiva *Earth Democracy: Justice, Sustainability, and Peace*. Cambridge, MA: South End, 2005.

Charles Tilly *Democracy*. New York: Cambridge University Press, 2007.

Cornell West *Democracy Matters: Winning the Fight Against Imperialism*. New York: Penguin, 2004.

Fareed Zakaria *The Future of Freedom: Illiberal Democracy at Home and Abroad*. New York: Norton, 2007.

# Index